ISRAEL
IN
EXILE

OVERTURES TO BIBLICAL THEOLOGY

Editors

WALTER BRUEGGEMANN, Professor of Old Testament at Columbia
  Theological Seminary, Decatur, Georgia

JOHN R. DONAHUE, S.J., Professor of New Testament at the Jesuit
  School of Theology, Berkeley, California

A
Theological
Interpretation

ISRAEL IN EXILE

RALPH W. KLEIN

FORTRESS PRESS   Philadelphia

Third printing 1988

Library of Congress Cataloging in Publication Data

Klein, Ralph W
  Israel in exile, a theological interpretation.

  (Overtures to Biblical theology)
  Includes index.
  1. Jews—History—Babylonian captivity, 598–515 B. C.
—Biblical teaching. 2. Exiles—Biblical teaching.
3. Bible. O. T.—Theology. I. Title. II. Series.
BS1199.B3K57   224   79-7382
ISBN 0–8006–1532–8

3629C88   Printed in the United States of America   1-1532

For
MARTHA and REBECCA
whose joy in life
mocks the darkness

Contents

Series Foreword

Biblical theology has been a significant part of modern study of the Jewish and Christian Scriptures. Prior to the ascendancy of historical criticism of the Bible in the nineteenth century, biblical theology was subordinated to the dogmatic concerns of the churches, and the Bible too often provided a storehouse of rigid proof texts. When biblical theology was cut loose from its moorings to dogmatic theology to become an enterprise seeking its own methods and categories, attention was directed to what the Bible itself had to say. A dogmatic concern was replaced by an historical one so that biblical theology was understood as an investigation of what was believed by different communities in different situations. By the end of the nineteenth century biblical theology was virtually equated with the history of the religion of the authors who produced biblical documents or of the communities which used them.

While these earlier perspectives have become more refined and sophisticated, they still describe the parameters of what is done in the name of biblical theology—moving somewhere between the normative statements of dogmatic theology and the descriptive concerns of the history of religions. Th. Vriezen, in his *An Outline of Old Testament Theology* (Dutch, 1949; ET, 1958), sought to combine these concerns by devoting the first half of his book to historical considerations and the second half to theological themes. But even that effort did not break out of the stalemate of categories. In more recent times Old Testament theology has been dominated by two paradigmatic works. In his *Theology of the Old Testament* (German, 1933–39; ET, 1967) W. Eichrodt has provided a comprehensive statement around fixed categories which reflect classical dogmatic interests, although the centrality of covenant in his work reflects the Bible's own categories. By contrast, G. von Rad in his *Old Testament Theology* (German, 1960; ET, 1965) has presented a study of theological traditions with a primary concern for the historical dynamism of the traditions. In the case of New Testament theology, historical and theological concerns are rather roughly juxtaposed in the work of A. Richardson, *An Introduction to the Theology of the New Testament*. As in the case of the Old Testament there are two major options or presentations which dominate in New Testament studies. The history-of-religion school has left its mark on the magisterial work of R. Bultmann, who proceeds from an explanation of the expressions of faith of the earliest communities and their theologians to a statement of how their understanding of existence under faith speaks to us today. The works of O. Cullmann and W. G. Kümmel are clear New Testament statements of *Heilsgeschichte* under the aegis of the tension between promise and fulfillment—categories reminiscent of von Rad.

As recently as 1962 K. Stendahl again underscored the tension between historical description and normative meaning by assigning to the biblical theologian the task of describing what the Bible *meant*, not what it *means* or *how* it can have meaning. However, this objectivity of historical description is too often found to be a mirror of the observer's hidden preunderstanding, and the adequacy of historical description is contingent on one generation's discoveries and postulates. Also, the yearning and expectation of believers and would-be believers will not let biblical theology rest with the descriptive task alone. The growing strength of Evangelical Protestantism and the expanding phenomenon of charismatic Catholicism are but vocal reminders that people seek in the Bible a source of alternative value systems. By its own character and by the place it occupies in our culture the Bible will not rest easy as merely an historical artifact.

Thus it seems a fitting time to make "overtures" concerning biblical theology. It is not a time for massive tomes which claim too much. It appears not even to be a time for firm conclusions which are too comprehensive. It is a time for pursuit of fresh hints, for exploration of new intuitions which may reach beyond old conclusions, set categories, and conventional methods. The books in this series are concerned not only with what is seen and heard, with what the Bible said, but also with what the Bible says and the ways in which seeing and hearing are done.

In putting forth these *Overtures* much remains unsettled. The certainties of the older biblical theology *in service* of dogmatics, as well as of the more recent biblical theology movement *in lieu* of dogmatics, are no longer present. Nor is there on the scene anyone of the stature of a von Rad or a Bultmann to offer a synthesis which commands the theological engagement of a generation and summons the church to a new restatement of the biblical message. In a period characterized by an information explosion the relation of analytic study to attempts at synthesis is unsettled. Also unsettled is the question whether the scholarly canon of the university or the passion of the confessing community provides a language and idiom of discourse, and equally unsettled—and unsettling—is the question whether biblical theology is simply one more specialization in an already fragmented study of Scripture or whether it is finally the point of it all.

But much remains clear. Not simply must the community of biblical scholars address fresh issues and articulate new categories for the well-being of our common professional task; equally urgent is the fact that the dominant intellectual tradition of the West seems now to carry less conviction and to satisfy only weakly the new measures of knowing which are among us. We do not know exactly what role the Bible will play in new theological statements or religious postures, nor what questions the Bible can and will address, but *Overtures* will provide a locus where soundings may be taken.

We not only intend that *Overtures* should make contact with people professionally involved in biblical studies, but hope that the series will speak to all who care about the heritage of the biblical tradition. We hope that the volumes will represent the best in a literary and historical study of biblical traditions without canonizing historical archaism. We hope also that the studies will be relevant without losing the mystery of biblical religion's historical distance, and that the studies touch on significant themes, motifs, and symbols of the Bible without losing the rich diversity of the biblical tradition. It is a time for normative literature which is not heavy-handed, but which seriously challenges not only our conclusions but also the shape of our questions.

Professor Klein, in the present volume, has addressed a theme receiving much attention in our current cultural climate. The theme of homelessness is now a pervasive one in a variety of disciplines. Exile is a symbol found increasingly powerful for the illumination of our present circumstance.

The motif is of peculiar pertinence now because we seem to be in an unprecedented situation. Now it is not only the economically disadvantaged or the politically oppressed who experience homelessness. Those judged by the world to be affluent, powerful, and free are also those who are "far from home." Klein brings together a variety of strands of current scholarship and offers his own sensitivity to Scripture to provide a fresh statement of biblical resources available for the current task and place of the church.

Among other things, Klein shows:

1. How the experience of exile touches both economic-political realities and the collapse of symbol systems. It is the linkage between symbols and the more concrete aspects of our life which creates a situation of deep homelessness.

2. That while the problem is recognized in Israel and generally agreed upon (how could it be otherwise in the sixth century?), the responses to it in the Old Testament, from both Babylon and Palestine, are rich and varied. Thus he fully honors the current stress on the fluidity and flexibility of biblical faith in response to cultural issues. The pain of Israel is too deep to admit only one response.

3. That while the crisis in Israel has many dimensions, exile finally must be faced in terms of God, God's freedom and faithfulness, God's power and inclination. In the context of modernity, we are sore tempted to define the problem and seek its solution on other grounds, but this much Israel never doubted.

WALTER BRUEGGEMANN
JOHN R. DONAHUE, S.J.

Abbreviations

AB	Anchor Bible
AnBib	Analecta biblica
ANET	J. B. Pritchard (ed.), *Ancient Near Eastern Texts*
BA	*Biblical Archaeologist*
BBB	Bonner biblische Beiträge
BHS	*Biblia hebraica stuttgartensia*
Bib	*Biblica*
BibLeb	*Bibel und Leben*
BibSt	Biblische Studien
BKAT	Biblischer Kommentar: Altes Testament
BWANT	Beiträge zur Wissenschaft vom Alten und Neuen Testament
BZ	*Biblische Zeitschrift*
BZAW	Beihefte zur *ZAW*
CBQ	*Catholic Biblical Quarterly*
FRLANT	Forschungen zur Religion und Literatur des Alten und Neuen Testaments
HAT	Handbuch zum Alten Testament
IDBSup	Supplementary Volume to *Interpreter's Dictionary of the Bible*
Int	*Interpretation*
JAOS	*Journal of the American Oriental Society*
JBL	*Journal of Biblical Literature*
JSOT	*Journal for the Study of the Old Testament*
KD	*Kerygma und Dogma*
LXX	Septuagint
MT	Masoretic Text

NCB	New Century Bible
OTL	Old Testament Library
RB	*Revue biblique*
TBü	Theologische Bücherei
TLZ	*Theologische Literaturzeitung*
TRu	*Theologische Rundschau*
VT	*Vetus Testamentum*
VTSup	Vetus Testamentum, Supplements
WMANT	Wissenschaftliche Monographien zum Alten und Neuen Testament
ZAW	*Zeitschrift für die alttestamentliche Wissenschaft*
ZTK	*Zeitschrift für Theologie und Kirche*

Preface

This book could not have been written without the stimulating contributions and questions of students who enrolled for my course "A Theology for Exiles" at Christ Seminary—Seminex. There never would have been time to organize these thoughts and get them down on paper without leave time made possible by the Association of Theological Schools, the Alexander von Humboldt Stiftung, and the Board of Directors of Christ Seminary—Seminex. Everyone at the Georgia Augusta Universität in Göttingen went out of their way to provide the best possible facilities for writing and research, including the staff of the theological library. Professor Walther Zimmerli, who served as my host for the Humboldt Stiftung, and Professors Hanhart, Perlitt, and Smend enriched me with their scholarship and their warm friendship and hospitality. Daily conversations with Assistant Hermann Spieckermann alerted me to much recent continental research and provided an invaluable foil for my own thinking.

The biblical translations, except in chapter 1, are from the RSV, although I have always rendered the divine name as Yahweh instead of LORD. When I have departed from the RSV, my initials appear by the citation of the biblical text. An asterisk after a verse number means that only part of that verse is involved. Abbreviations follow the guidelines of the *Journal of Biblical Literature* 95 (1976) : 339–46.

Introduction—
Making the Most
of Disaster

Israel's Exile as Catalyst

When the Babylonian armies conquered Judah in the early sixth century B.C., they unleashed a host of physical and socio-economic problems. Already in 597 Nebuchadnezzar exiled from Judah King Jehoiachin, members of the royal family, nobles, landowners, military leaders, elders, craftsmen, priests, and prophets. While these people numbered only ten thousand men or less (2 Kings 24:14, 16; Jer. 52:28), they came from the leadership class and their loss represented a severe blow to the southern kingdom. We date the beginning of the Exile to this first deportation.

The ten years after 597 found Judah living under Zedekiah, the uncle of Jehoiachin. In 589 or 588 this weak puppet king revolted against his Babylonian overlords, leading Nebuchadnezzar to besiege Jerusalem. About two years later the city fell, King Zedekiah was captured as he attempted to flee, the temple was burned, and additional people were exiled. When Gedaliah, the governor appointed by the Babylonians, was assassinated, many citizens of Judah and Benjamin fled to Egypt, taking the prophet Jeremiah with them. We read of a third deportation in 582 (Jer. 52:30) and the release of King Jehoiachin in 561 (2 Kings 25:27–30), but otherwise the Bible is relatively silent about historical events until Cyrus, the first king of the Persian Empire, captured Babylon in 539 and permitted some of the Jews to return home to Palestine. For our purposes the fall of Babylon in 539 will serve as the final event of the exilic period.[1]

Exile meant death, deportation, destruction, and devastation. How many died in all is fully unknown, but the siege had its victims of starvation, and many others died in battle. Some fled or hid in caves (Jer. 40:11–12). The exact size of the deportation is unknown since the Bible's figures conflict with one another (cf. 2 Kings 24:14, 16; Jer. 52:28) and since we do not know whether the figures included wives and children or not. The deportation had a significant socioeconomic and psychological impact, not least because of the caliber of the people who were exiled. The group was large enough in any case to initiate an ongoing Jewish presence in Babylon. Jerusalem was systematically destroyed and so were a number of other Judean cities.[2]

Despite the efforts of contemporary biblical research, much remains unknown about the socioeconomic conditions in Palestine and in Babylon during the Exile, about the worship of the two communities, about the renewed importance apparently assumed by Sabbath and circumcision in this period, and about the origins of the synagogue, often thought to have begun in the sixth century. The Bible provides only passing references to contemporary institutions (e.g. to the elders in Babylon, Ezek. 14:1; 20:1) or permits only an indirect reconstruction of the contemporary situation (e.g. the polemic against the gods in Second Isaiah presupposes that these gods were a serious challenge to the Jews in Babylon).

A substantial number of people continued to live in Palestine, though the archaeological finds indicate the land was underoccupied and impoverished. While this Palestinian remnant

1. A number of excellent historical surveys of the Exile are available: Peter R. Ackroyd, *Exile and Restoration* (Philadelphia: Westminster Press, 1968), pp. 17–38; idem, *Israel under Babylon and Persia* (London: Oxford University Press, 1970), pp. 1–59; John Bright, *A History of Israel* (Philadelphia: Westminster Press, 1972), pp. 343–60; and Burtenay Oded in *Israelite and Judean History*, ed. J. H. Hayes and J. M. Miller (Philadelphia: Westminster Press, 1977), pp. 469–88.

2. Oded, *Israelite History*, p. 475, lists Lachish, Tell Zakariya (Azekah), Eglon, Tell Beth Mirsim, Tell el-Ful, Beth Zur, Ramat Rachel, Beth-Shemesh, Bethel, Arad, Ein Gedi, and others.

never went *into* exile, the exilic hardships and their challenge to
the faith were surely theirs. A good part of the "exilic" literature
was, in fact, produced in Palestine.[3]
Not much more is known of conditions in Babylon. Ackroyd
speaks of reasonable freedom, settlement in communities, the
possibility of marriage, the people's ordering of their own affairs,
and relative prosperity.[4] We know that communication between
Palestine and Babylon was possible (cf. Jeremiah's letter to the
exiles). Some have detected a growing bitterness as the Exile wore
on (cf. Isa. 13—14; Jer. 50—51; Isa. 46—47).

To think of either group as prisoners of war or to compare
their situation with the concentration camps of our century
would be misleading if not wrong. Exilic Israel nevertheless was
a defeated nation that had lost its independence, its land, its
monarchy, and its temple. There had been abundant pain and
death, and it is hard to imagine that the economy was not completely topsy-turvy. Exile meant a host of physical and socio-
economic problems.

But the *theological* challenges and problems strike us as much
more severe. First, the temple in Jerusalem had been burned.
From our safe distance we may view the temple as a mixed blessing. Considered the footstool of God (Lam. 2:1), Yahweh's dwelling place (1 Kings 8:13; Ezek. 43:7), his resting place (Ps. 132:14),
or the place where his face was to be seen (Isa. 1:12 *BHS*), it had
also opened the door to Canaanite influences and to the notion
that God was the guarantor of the status quo. Though controversial, the temple was a tangible symbol of the people's election and
a reminder of God's unfailing actions in history on their behalf.
Now that temple had gone up in flames, and enemies had raced
through the sanctuary in which foreigners were not even to be
present (Lam. 1:10; Deut. 23:3–4). Worst of all, the temple's
destruction called God into question: either there were deities

3. The best discussion of this Palestinian group and its theological contribution is that of E. Janssen, *Juda in der Exilszeit*, FRLANT 69 (Göttingen:
Vandenhoeck & Ruprecht, 1956).
4. Ackroyd, *Exile and Restoration*, p. 32. Cf. Oded, *Israelite History*, pp.
480–86.

stronger than or superior to Yahweh, or for some reason Yahweh had rejected his own people and his own place.

Secondly, the end of the Davidic dynasty was a theological problem. Had not Yahweh promised an eternal dynasty to David (2 Sam. 7)? Did not the royal psalms view him as God's adopted son (Ps. 2:7) and as the medium through whom Yahweh's blessings were channeled to the people (Ps. 72:6 and 16)? Had there not been in fact great kings—Asa, Hezekiah, and especially Josiah —who demonstrated the promise's validity? Kings had come and gone, but kingship itself and the state had endured through thick and thin. Now Zedekiah had been captured, his two sons had been murdered before his eyes, and then he had been blinded. His nephew, Jehoiachin, king himself for only three months in 597, sat in a Babylonian prison. What did all this mean for the trustworthiness of the God of the Davidic promise? If he were to be considered faithful, it could only be because he had judged and rejected kingship as practiced.

Or consider the land. The promises of land and descendants were the key items from the patriarchal tradition. Yahweh was the owner of the land, and his gift of the land to Israel was hailed by the Deuteronomist and by the psalmists, among others. The land, Israel's inheritance, was now in the hands of foreigners. Why was Yahweh not keeping this promise? Was he too weak, or had he become so angry with his people?

The covenant of Sinai offered a choice between life and blessing or death and curse as late as the time of the Deuteronomist. When Josiah discovered the book of the law, he had recognized at once how desperately close the curse was. But with 597 and 587 the curses of the covenant had in fact fallen on Israel; the Sinai covenant could no longer be the basis for exhortation and for a positive option. The covenant had been broken by Israel (Jer. 31:32).

The same kinds of dilemmas were posed by the decimation of the priesthood through exile and execution and by the cessation of sacrifices. How could Yahweh's songs ever be sung in a foreign land (Ps. 137:4)? And what about the recital of Yahweh's saving deeds? What hope for the future did they offer? His power in the Exodus from Egypt, his beneficence in the conquest, his repeated righteous triumphs in Israel's more than six centuries in the land (Judg. 5:11) appeared either as irrelevant, past, and no longer adequate evidence for Yahweh's reign, or they could be used in indictments of Israel's infidelity.

In short, almost all of the old symbol systems had been rendered useless. Almost all of the old institutions no longer functioned. What kind of future was possible for a people which traced its unique election to a God who had just lost a war to other deities? What kind of future was possible for a people who had so alienated their God that categorical rejection was his necessary response?

Israel's responses to exile reflect the immensity of the disaster. A poet could cry out with nostalgic longing and self-imprecation:

> If I forget you, O Jerusalem,
>   let my right hand wither!
> Let my tongue cleave to the roof of my mouth,
>   if I do not remember you,
>   if I do not set Jerusalem above my highest joy!
>   (Ps. 137:5–6)

But the same poem continues with bloodcurdling curses against the opportunistic Edomites and the conquering Babylonians:

> Happy shall he be who takes your little ones
>   and dashes them against the rock!
>   (v. 9)

Doubt too emerged in those days. Had Josiah perhaps erred in closing down the local sanctuaries or in abolishing the worship of other deities (cf. Jer. 44:18)? The Deuteronomistic polemic against Canaanite religion was in part an indictment for past misdeeds. It is not difficult to imagine, however, that it was directed also to current problems in the Exile when recourse to the old "other gods" was one reaction of those who doubted. Recourse to the victor's "new gods" was another response. Second Isaiah reports Yahweh's lawsuits against them, in which their claims of power and even of existence are shown to be worthless. That he was not tilting at windmills can be seen already in

Ezekiel's citation of the people's response: "Let us be like the nations, like the tribes of the countries, and worship wood and stone" (20:32). To doubt could be added despair: "Our bones are dried up, our hope is lost; we are clean cut off" (Ezek. 37:11).

In frustration Israel turned to direct accusation: Yahweh is behaving like an enemy, mobilizing his weapons of war against his own people (Lam. 2:4–5). What a contrast with the confession that Yahweh's hand, his arm, and the light of his face had brought about the conquest victories (Ps. 44:3–4).

Others responded to the Exile by protesting their own innocence. They complained that the fathers' sins were visited on the innocent children (Jer. 31:29; Ezek. 18:2) or that the sin of some (kings and other apostates) brought Yahweh's anger on all (cf. Pss. 44:17–18; 79:8).

Not all responses were negative, but even these positive responses underscore the depths of the theological problem and the uncertainty about the correct way into the future. When everything seemed to be changing, one could appeal for a return to the oldest promises and the Mosaic ideal (the Priestly writing), or one could discount the past and talk of the necessity of brand new saving acts of Yahweh (Second Isaiah). The heightened stress on circumcision in exilic and postexilic texts and the renewed interest in the Sabbath can easily be understood as attempts to maintain a separate identity as an elect people in an alien culture, a culture in which assimilation seemed to offer more chance for success. To some it was a time for confessing guilt, for acknowledging the complete justification of Yahweh's actions, and for turning to Yahweh (Deuteronomistic History; cf. Lam. 1:18). In such a situation, is it any wonder that others responded with renewed stress on God's forgiveness (Jer. 31:34; Ezekiel; Second Isaiah; P; cf. Mic. 7:7–20)? Finally, some responded with almost uncontrollable grief. To articulate sorrow over physical and theological problems brought catharsis. For others deep expressions of sorrow were a way to move Yahweh into action (Lam. 2:18–21). Or could suffering itself be redemptive? To bear the reversals of history silently as Yahweh's servant, trusting in him alone—would not this be a way to let the nations see the grandeur of Yahweh even in punishment (the servant poems in Second Isaiah; cf. Jeremiah)?

Which was the way out of or beyond exile? In this book we propose to describe six literary works from the period of the Exile: the exilic laments (the Book of Lamentations and selected Psalms); the Deuteronomistic History; the prophets Jeremiah, Ezekiel, and Second Isaiah; and the Priestly writing in the Pentateuch. In these writings we will see that the depths of the Exile were the occasion for some of the most profound insights in the entire Old Testament. These writers made the most of a disaster.

Some of these writings show little hope or a highly restrained blueprint for the future (Lamentations, Deuteronomistic History; in part, Jeremiah); others, at least in their present form, contain explicit descriptions of what the future will or should be like (Ezekiel, Second Isaiah, the Priestly writing). The first three works are probably the products of the Palestinian community; the latter three most likely emerged in Babylon.

We will seek to describe how the Exile shaped the entire message and outlook of these exilic authors. For each "book" we will ask, How is this book a response to exile or an analysis of it? How does reading the book with a sensitivity to the problems of the Exile open up new dimensions of the book or give it a new coherence? What new ideas are invoked by a given author? What old traditions? What is the central point around which his response to exile turns?

When one discusses biblical writings from within the "faith," one expects to find authoritative and meaningful words from God. As one reads these six exilic voices, such expectations are not disappointed by reality. But it is not only that the "answers" are powerful; it is also that the questions posed by the exilic age or perceived by the biblical writers were so acute and so modern —questions of identity and the grounds for hope, questions about who or what is the cause of Israel's malaise, questions about the continuing validity of symbols and symbol systems, questions for and in a time of radical change, questions for those who are rootless or whose future seems fruitless and fraught with conflict.

Israel's exilic theologians made the most of their disaster. They spoke to the types of questions that challenge academic theologians, the clergy, and the nonprofessional faithful also today. We can read Israel's exilic literature for help in making the most of our disasters. We hope and believe that we can learn from this literature, that by analogy to it and by adaptation of it we can yet speak and live for God, for other people, and for the world. The following six chapters primarily describe how six writers responded to an exile some twenty-five centuries ago. But we are called to use these resources to respond creatively and faithfully to today's "exilic" challenges as well. In the conclusion we will make a down payment on this hermeneutical task.

CHAPTER 1

Yahweh,

King and Enemy

Reactions to the Exile in
Lamentations and Other
Exilic Psalms

LAMENTATIONS

The book of Lamentations consists of five poems, mostly of an alphabetic acrostic type.[1] They come from early in the Exile and may have been used at public ceremonies on the site of the ruined temple,[2] though naturally this setting can only be advanced as one possibility among others. Whether written by one person or several we cannot say, but one person surely was responsible for the present arrangement of the book. To simplify the discussion we shall always speak of the author in the singular below.

Expressions of Horror and Grief

The author of Lamentations was obviously familiar with the harsh events of Jerusalem's final siege and the miseries of life in the land after 587, and he articulated his grief over many phases of this devastation.

1. In chaps. 1 and 2 each stanza contains three lines. The first line in each stanza begins with aleph, the second with beth, and so on. Chap. 4 is similar, but has only two lines per stanza. In chap. 3 each stanza has three lines and all three begin with the appropriate letter. Chap. 5 is not an alphabetic acrostic, but it does have twenty-two lines, corresponding to the number of letters in the Hebrew alphabet.
2. Cf. Zech. 7:1–5; 8:18–19; Jer. 41:5–6.

a. The scorn of the enemy. One need read only a few lines of Lamentations to sense the deep humiliation Israel experienced at the hand of the victorious enemy: "Her [Jerusalem's] enemies saw her and laughed at her collapse" (1:7).[3] "Yahweh, look upon my misery, at the insolence of the enemy!" (1:9). "All my enemies heard of my trouble; they rejoiced that you [Yahweh] had done it" (1:21). Enemy nations, who had been denied entry into the sanctuary in Israelite law (Deut. 23:3), now "entered" the temple, not to worship but to pillage (1:10). The enemy nations whistled, shook their heads, and threw Israel's praise of Zion back into their teeth (2:15; cf. 3:45–46).

b. The anguish of the elect. What made the scorn of the enemy especially hard to bear was that it was directed against a people who prided themselves in God's special care, his election. The "glory of Israel" had now fallen from heaven to earth (2:1), and the poet reminded God about the people's erstwhile rank: "Look, Yahweh, and consider whom you have treated so" (2:20). The sons of Zion, once considered so precious, were not thrown away like cheap pottery (4:2). Israel's special land (*naḥălâ*) had been given to strangers and foreigners (5:2). This was not any old land; it was the land of promise, the fruit of exodus and conquest, the gift of Yahweh's favor. Inviolable Zion, a favorite theme in the songs of Zion, was now just another heap of ruins. The kings of the earth couldn't believe that Jerusalem could fall, and no wonder: according to Israel's cult poetry the nations who plotted against Jerusalem were always vanquished (Pss. 46:6–7; 48:4–6; 76:3–5, 12). Now these same nations witnessed to and participated in Jerusalem's fall.

c. The scope of the destruction. The fires[4] and other means of destruction ruined things near and dear. The city itself (1:1; 2:15), its gates (1:4; 2:9; 4:12; 5:14), and its walls (2:7, 8, 18) lay in ruins. Even more serious from a theological standpoint was the damage done to the sanctuary (1·10; 2:7, 20) and its altar

---

3. Except where noted, the translations are from Delbert R. Hillers, *Lamentations*, AB 7A (Garden City, NY: Doubleday & Co., 1972).
4. 1:13; 2:3, 4; 4:11. Yahweh, not Babylon, is always said to be the author of these destructive fires.

(2:7), the loss of the temple treasures (1:10), and the cessation of the feasts, including the Sabbath (1:4; 2:6, 7). The temple had been considered God's footstool, where he was uniquely present, but that special honor had been flagrantly disregarded on Jerusalem's day of reckoning (2:1). Mt. Zion, in fact, had become the prowling place for foxes; it was ruined, under a curse (5:18). For many the Davidic king had been the source of nationalistic hopes. He was the channel by which God gave prosperity and life to the people (Ps. 72:6, 16). But Zedekiah, the last of the kings, was captured, blinded, and hauled off to die in exile. Nowhere else does the Bible use higher titles for the king than in our poet's anguished lament over the end of Zedekiah:

> The breath of our nostrils, the anointed of Yahweh, was caught
> in their traps,
> The one of whom we said, "In his shadow we will live among
> the nations."
>
> (4:20)

The king, accordingly, is the life breath of the people, an attribute elsewhere ascribed to God alone (Gen. 2:7; Ps. 104:29), and Yahweh's highly honored messiah. He is even compared with the tree that gives God-like protection (Pss. 17:8; 91:1; cf. Isa. 30:2-3). But now he is just another deposed kinglet, caught like an animal in the enemy's trap.

d. Famine and starvation. Modern warfare may outstrip that of the ancients in atrocity, but living in a city under siege had horrors all its own—and the worst of them was starvation. The poet laments the fact that dignified people had to search through garbage cans for food (4:5) and that mothers bartered their children for a bite to eat (1:11). Those killed by the sword could consider themselves lucky; others starved to death (4:9; cf. 5:6, 9, 10). Deeply touching is the picture of mothers' helpless responses to their starving children's pleas (2:11-12; cf. 4:3-4). But the worst result of famine was cannibalism: mothers ate their own children in a desperate attempt to stay alive (2:20; 4:9-10). No wonder the poet considered his pain incomparable (1:12; cf. 2:13).

The Theological Dimensions of the Disaster

a. Yahweh is the enemy. The ranks of Babylon's soldiers were the tools, but Yahweh was the real instigator of Jerusalem's disaster. After describing how her young men and women lie fallen, Zion expresses her grief in a complaint against Yahweh:

> You killed them on the day of your wrath;
> you slaughtered them without mercy.
>
> (2:21)

Yahweh had become an enemy (v. 5). Worse yet, this was his plan, carried out with methodical, deliberate, and unrelenting thoroughness (2:8) in fulfillment of his frequently announced threats (2:17). Chap. 3 pictures Yahweh as a perverse shepherd: "He led and guided me into darkness, not light" (v. 2; per contra Ps. 23:1). Yahweh wrapped himself in a cloud that effectively blocked off all prayers to him (3:44; cf. 3:8). What happened to Jerusalem in 587 was not merely Nebuchadnezzar putting a final end to Jerusalem's fickle foreign policy; it was Yahweh's merciless day of wrath (1:12; 2:1, 22).[5] Four times Lamentations notes that God tore down or slew "without sparing" (2:2, 17, 21; 3:43). He pursued Israel like a veritable hound of heaven (3:43). Yahweh simply forgot and abandoned Israel (5:20); he remembered neither his temple (2:1) nor his people's terrible suffering (5:1ff.).

b. We are the sinners. The poet employs a rich vocabulary to make clear that Jerusalem's sin is the real cause of the destruction.[6] Words of confession are put into the mouth of the people (5:7, 16; 3:42) and of Zion (1:18, 20, 22). The people concede that their sins only continued what their fathers had done and that their punishment is well deserved (5:7, 16; per contra Jer. 31:29–30; Ezek. 18:2). Nevertheless, the book is not very specific about the identity of that sin. One can of course say that the noun *peša'* (1:5) often means rebellion against a suzerain (cf. 2 Kings 1:1) and may imply transgression against the covenant Lord, but

---

5. The writer employs six different nouns (*'ap, ḥārôn, ḥārî, ḥēmâ, za'am, 'ebrâ*) some eighteen times to express the wrathful character of God's judgment.

6. The nouns *peša', 'awôn, ḥēṭ',* and *ḥaṭṭā'â;* the verbs *ḥāṭā', pāša',* and *mārâ.*

the term *covenant* is lacking in the entire book. The poet, in any case, has no doubt about the immensity of the people's sin: it was greater than Sodom's (4:6). He scores the reliance on foreign alliances during the final crisis as well as in earlier times (4:17; 5:6; cf. Hos. 7:11; 11:5; Jer. 2:18, 36; 37:5–10).

Significantly, the poet holds the religious leaders to be the chief sinners (2:14). The prophets and priests shed within Jerusalem the blood of innocent men (4:13). This charge is not altogether implausible in view of the priests' activities in an earlier period (Hos. 6:9) or in view of the attitude of the religious establishment toward Jeremiah (chap. 26), but perhaps the author of Lamentations only means to assert that the religious leaders were responsible for the rulers' (cf. 2 Kings 21:16) or the people's (Jer. 7:6) violence in that they winked at their injustice (2:14).

An extensive accounting for sin would be necessary, perhaps, only if God's justice were in question. But in this book Zion raises no complaint about God's fairness: "Yahweh is in the right, for I disobeyed his command" (1:18).

Resolution of Grief; Hope

Lamentations was written in the shadows of Jerusalem's fall and its attendant grief. The poet found no hope in the traditions of the fathers, the Exodus, the land, Zion, or David, nor does he speak of a new exodus or the like.[7] Yet his message is not exhausted in articulating grief and guilt. He offers a restrained hope.

In certain respects his limited outlook toward the future forms an important foil to the more exuberant message of Second Isaiah at the other end of the Exile. Zion's frequent complaint that there is no one to comfort her (Lam. 1:2, 9, 16, 17, 21) differs

7. Cf. Hillers, *Lamentations*, p. XVI. Bertil Albrektson (*Studies in the Text and Theology of the Book of Lamentations*, Studia Theologica Lundensia 21 [Lund: CWK Gleerup, 1963], pp. 214–39) has identified the presence of cultic traditions in the poems, including Zion's inviolability, the election of David, and the kingship of Yahweh, and he proposes that these traditions were used to express the book's diagnosis of the problem, the tension between faith and reality. The poet used a Deuteronomistic way of thinking, on the other hand, when he saw the events of 587 as God's judgment or curse (cf. Deut. 28) or the fulfillment of the prophetic word.

dramatically from the opening words of Second Isaiah: "Comfort, comfort my people" (Isa. 40:1). Zion's ruin for this author is beyond compare; there is no analogy that could be invoked for her consolation (2:13; cf. 1:12). There is simply no healing (2:13; cf. 2 Chron. 36:16).

At times the poet expresses himself in ways that anticipate themes in Second Isaiah without fully attaining their positive content. "Your punishment (*'ăwōnēk*) is complete, O Zion! He will not exile you again" (4:22). With the fall of Jerusalem, in other words, the worst of Israel's days had passed. For Second Isaiah too the worst days were over, but he went on to speak of forgiveness for the people's iniquity and of the sufficiency of Jerusalem's suffering (40:2). A petition in Lamentations echoes Second Isaiah, but from afar:

> Be near when I call you; tell me not to be afraid.
> Lord, be on my side in this struggle; redeem my life.
>   (3:57–58)

What Jerusalem can only pray for in Lamentations is surpassed by the *fear nots* of Second Isaiah's oracles of salvation and by his frequent assurances that Yahweh has redeemed.

The resolution of grief also depends on Yahweh's vindication of himself over against the neighboring nations. Without denying her own rebellion or questioning the basic justice of her fate, Zion insists that divine justice requires Yahweh to deal as severely with the nations' wickedness as with hers:

> Oh bring on the day you proclaimed and let them be like me!
> Let all their wickedness come before you, and do to them
> Just what you did to me for all my rebellions.
>   (1:21–22)

The poet develops this theme at length in 3:52–66. Here the surrounding nations, rather than Yahweh, are viewed as the enemy (v. 52; per contra 2:5). They have brought Zion to the depths, and she needs God's support against them in court (v. 59). Because Yahweh pursued Israel in anger (v. 43), he now is asked to pursue the nations with the selfsame anger (v. 66) and wipe them out: "Give them back, Yahweh, what they have coming, for what their hands have done" (v. 64).

Every Morning Mercies New

Chap. 3 forms a major building block in the poet's attempt to resolve his sorrow. The first sixteen verses contain the complaints of a sufferer, perhaps a model sufferer, who feels put upon by God. Despite the speaker's sickness and imprisonment, God has denied his prayer and acted like a lurking bear and a bully. The sufferer is the object of everyone's ridicule. Small wonder that in vv. 17–20 he sinks in despair.

And yet one thing gives him hope and on that alone he sets his heart: Yahweh's mercies never come to an end,[8] and his pity is never exhausted (v. 22). What the poet remembers is not the specific traditions of the covenant, the Exodus, the promises to David, or the gift of the land. Rather, he recalls the merciful *character* of God. Compare the oft used cultic formula: "Yahweh, Yahweh, a God merciful and gracious, slow to anger and abounding in steadfast love and faithfulness" (Exod. 34:6; cf. Num. 14: 18; Neh. 9:17, 31; Pss. 86:15; 103:8; 145:8; Jer. 32:18; Joel 2:13; Jon. 4:2).[9] The gracious kindnesses God has shown to his people are new every morning. They are new in the sense that they are not worn out or used up.[10] Yahweh himself is the portion allotted to the poet, just as he was the portion allotted to Aaron in lieu of land (Num. 18:20; cf. Ps. 73:26).

Since God's help is abiding, the poet concludes that God is always good to those who hope in him or seek him (v. 25). Silent hoping in God, however, must be matched by silent acceptance of suffering, accepting its blows and reproaches (vv. 27–29). Yet this is acceptance of suffering in view of release from it: (a) Yahweh

---

8. For the text see *BHS*. Cf. 4:22 where we are told that the punishment for Zion's iniquity does come to an end.
9. Cf. Phyllis Trible, *God and the Rhetoric of Sexuality* (Philadelphia: Fortress Press, 1978), pp. 1–4.
10. Cf. Job 29:20: "My honor is (always) 'new' with me; and my bow ever fresh in my hand" (RWK).

does not reject forever (v. 31); (*b*) after he afflicts he has pity in accordance with his mercies (v. 32; cf. v. 22); (*c*) God's tormenting of men is his "strange work," it does not come from his heart (v. 33).

Because God's governance of the world is (in the final analysis) good (vv. 37–38), one who suffers should not complain about what his sins have brought on him (v. 39). This thought brings a surprise ending to the lament of vv. 1–39. The "ideal sufferer" has moved from complaint about unfair suffering to despair and to hope in God's unfailing mercy. In his hope he waits on God and submits to suffering, trusting that God always replaces affliction with mercy, or at least that it is part of his sovereign freedom to do so.[11] Having affirmed the goodness of God, the poet now calls his own goodness into question.

On the basis of this paradigmatic lament (vv. 1–39), the nation is called to self-examination and sincere repentance (vv. 40–41). The people respond in v. 42 with a confession of their sins. It is their unforgiven sins which have led to God's killing without sparing (v. 43), to his deafness to prayers (v. 44), to the mockery of the enemies (vv. 45–46), and to the people's utter ruin (v. 47).

The poet plans to cry unceasingly over this ruin until Yahweh looks down from heaven and sees (vv. 48–50).[12] Similarly, Zion is urged in 2:19 to cry to Yahweh amidst her tears: "Look, Yahweh, and consider whom you have treated so" (2:20). The crying of Zion (1:2, 16 and 2:19) and of the poet (2:11; 3:48–50) must be seen not only as expressions of grief, as emotional catharsis— though they surely are that. They are also designed to attract God's attention to Zion's plight. When Yahweh finally sees, he will replace Zion's affliction with his own pity. The insights gained in the individual psalm of lament (vv. 1–39)—that God's mercies and pity are "new" and never exhausted—form the basis for hope for grief-stricken Zion. Crying, of course, is not enough.

---

11. God's freedom seems to be underscored by the "maybe" (*'ûlay*) of v. 29. Cf. Amos 5:15 and Zeph. 2:3.
12. Cf. 1:9, 11, 20; 3:59–60; 5:1. Cf. Hos. 12:4 where Jacob's weeping is understood as a way to ask for God's blessing.

Self-evaluation and sincere repentance must follow even if these actions too are brought about by God's answer to prayer:

> Bring us back to you, Yahweh, and we will return,
> Make our days as they were before.
>
> (5:21)

Faith in the Depths

The final and in many ways the most poignant expression of hope comes in chap. 5. The poet moves through a series of vivid pictures of the disaster, including the loss of land, the terrible famine, rape, assassination, forced labor, and streets without joy. Heartsick he laments, "On Mount Zion, which lies desolate, foxes prowl about" (5:18). Is this the city they call the perfection of beauty (cf. 2:15)? Is Mount Zion really the city of the great king (Ps. 48:2)? Does God really shine forth from *this* Zion (Ps. 50:2)? The prowling foxes seem to represent more than scavengers among fallen stones. In the ancient Near East they were also a sign of God's curse.[13]

Precisely at this nadir of emotion and theology the poet dares to confess:

> But you, Yahweh, sit enthroned forever;
> Your throne lasts generation after generation.
>
> (5:19 RWK)

God's everlasting kingship is affirmed in spite of a destroyed Jerusalem and a Zion under curse. During the Exile Ezekiel and Second Isaiah appealed to God's kingship as displayed in the new exodus, as we shall see, and Psalms 74 and 102 took heart from God's kingship as shown in creation. In Lamentations, however, the poet restricts himself to a simple reaffirmation of God's everlasting kingship. God's kingship was part of his character, repeatedly affirmed in Israel's worship (e.g. Pss. 9:7, 11; 99:1). It is now the one hope for return and renewal (Lam. 5:21). Yet the

---

13. Cf. *ANET*, p. 651, ll. 254–55, and the discussion in Hillers, *Lamentations*, pp. 100, 105.

book closes with no happy ending. The sad situation that required the saying of these laments still prevailed. For the first and only time the poet uses the *why* otherwise so frequent in Israel's laments:

> Why have you forgotten us forever?
> Why have you abandoned us for so many days?[14]
>
> (5:20 RWK)

PSALMS

Psalm 44[15]

The psalmist meditates on an inexplicable paradox: At the time of the conquest it was God's power alone which won the victory, and Israel consistently praised Yahweh for his salvation in the fathers' days. Despite such trust and innocence, however, Israel has been defeated, and God appears powerless to help. He even seems to fight *against* Israel.

Israel complains that God has rejected them (v. 9; cf. 74:1; 77:7; and Lam. 3:31), slaughtered and scattered them (v. 11), and made them an object of the nations' ridicule (vv. 13–16). Though nations really want to attack Yahweh, they take out their hostility on Israel instead. The people complain, "For your sake, O God, we are killed all the day long" (v. 22).

Israel prays to a God who seems to be sleeping (v. 23; cf. Ps. 121:4); the agonized *why* in vv. 23–24 is an accusation against God who hides his face. In Israel's early days the light of God's face brought victories (v. 3). Now God has forgotten Israel's affliction and oppression (v. 24).

Over against this record of rejection, the people protest their innocence: we have not forgotten God and we have not been false to his covenant (v. 17), either by forgetting his name or by

14. Lothar Perlitt, "Anklage und Freispruch Gottes," *ZTK* 69 (1972) : 290–303, suggests that behind such a formalized question lies the voice of people who asserted it as a fact or accusation.
15. This psalm can be dated to the Exile by the following data: (*a*) Israel's armies have been beaten (v. 9) ; (*b*) her foes have plundered her (v. 10) ; (*c*) many people have been killed while others have been scattered among the nations (vv. 11–12; cf. 106:27) ; (*d*) her neighbors view her with scorn (vv. 13–16).

worshiping foreign gods (v. 20). On the contrary, the people praise God all day long (v. 8). Such a protestation of innocence, though in part merely a standard feature in Israel's laments, stands in remarkable tension to the notion that exile resulted from a broken covenant (Jer. 31:32) and to the notion attested elsewhere that exile is the result of sin. Are these the words of a group in Jerusalem that distinguished itself from the wicked people who were exiled, or from the sins of their fathers? Would they have shared in the cynicism which said, "The fathers have eaten sour grapes, and the children's teeth are set on edge" (Jer. 31:29; Ezek. 18:2)?

Since the attitude of God seems inconsistent and unfair, the people cry out for God to rouse himself and wake up (v. 23), to help and redeem (v. 26). Why should he? The people ask God to act for the sake of his "mercy" (*hasdekā,* v. 26)—a striking parallel to the appeal to God's never-ending mercies (*hasdé*) in Lam. 3:22 (cf. Isa. 55:3).

Psalm 74[16]

As in Psalm 44, we have no mention of the people's guilt in this psalm (cf. v. 19), and the prayer for God to regard his covenant (v. 20) presupposes that its promises are still valid and functional. The central concern of this community lament is God's inexplicable rejection of his elect people (vv. 2, 19). Especially disconcerting has been the noise of the enemy in God's sanctuary, their violent destruction of its interior (however vv. 5 and 6 are to be translated), and their burning the temple to the ground (v. 7). These enemies scoff at God and revile his name (vv. 10, 18, 22, 23). Yet, complains the psalmist, God stands mutely by, his hands tucked inside his garment (v. 11). God rejects his own people and is angry with them; he seems helplessly unmoved by the slanders of his enemies.

Yet the people who first prayed this psalm found a resolution

16. The most important evidence for dating this psalm comes in the reference to the burning of the temple in v. 7. Cf. the terminology similar to P in vv. 2–4. An exilic date is defended by J. J. M. Roberts, "Of Signs, Prophets, and Time Limits: A Note on Ps. 74:9," *CBQ* 39 (1977): 474–81.

for their complaint and a basis for their petitions in the confession of God's eternal kingship (vv. 12–17). This kingship manifested itself in the victories of creation,[17] which are described in mythological language: at creation God defeated Yam, broke the heads of the dragons and Leviathan, and established earth's orders. The worshipers were not unaware of their own needs (cf. vv. 1, 2, and 19), but their prime concern seems to be the need for God's damaged honor to be defended:

> Arise, O God, plead thy cause;
> remember how the impious scoff at thee all the day.
> (v. 22; cf. vv. 7, 10, and 18)

Psalm 79[18]

The complaint against the nations in this psalm centers on their entrance into Yahweh's heritage (the land), their defilement of the temple, and their destruction of Jerusalem (v. 1). They have killed numerous people and left the unburied bodies of the elect as food for the carrion birds and the wild animals (vv. 2–3; cf. Deut. 28:26; 2 Sam. 21:10; Jer. 7:33). The worshipers bewail their own condition as objects of mockery (v. 4), but their most bitter complaint involves Yahweh himself, who has used the nations as the tools of his judgment:

> How long will you be angry, Yahweh, forever?
> How long will your jealousy burn like fire?
> (v. 5; RWK)

The psalm's petitions ask for judgment on the nations but deliverance and forgiveness for Israel, and they suggest many reasons why God should act. First, Yahweh is asked to pour out his wrath on those nations who neither know him nor invoke his name (v. 6) and who have poured out his people's blood (v. 10;

17. Ps. 44 also confessed the kingship of Yahweh and the victories he ordered, though the victories there are the triumphs of Jacob-Israel over its historical enemies. On the motif see Ralph W. Klein, "A Theology for Exiles—The Kingship of Yahweh," *Dialog* 17 (1978) : 128–34.
18. This community lament can be dated to the Exile because it reports the desecration of the temple and the slaughter of many people in and around Jerusalem (vv. 1–3).

cf. vv. 3 and 7). Israel does not here question its own punishment but, as in Lamentations, insists that the justice of God must also be meted out to the nations who have acted wickedly. In a second series of petitions the worshipers ask Yahweh not to remember the sins of the fathers because of his pity (v. 8); he should forgive their sins in order to defend his reputation (v. 9; cf. v. 10). Finally, the worshipers ask deliverance from threatened death on the basis of their prisonerlike groans (v. 11; cf. 102:21). God's great strength provides reason to expect a great deliverance (v. 11).

Psalm 102[19]

This poem consists of an *individual* lament (vv. 1–11 and 23–24) and a song of praise for Yahweh's power and mercy (vv. 12–22) and for his sure help (vv. 26–29).

The lament begins with typical, stylized complaints about the psalmist's own physical sufferings and the attacks of enemies. Both of these troubles have their ultimate basis in Yahweh's anger (v. 10). Though the psalmist is deeply aware of the transitoriness of life, he finds comfort in Yahweh's everlasting kingship (vv. 11–12). He goes on to confess that King Yahweh will rebuild Jerusalem (v. 16) out of pity and grace (v. 13). In this rebuilt Jerusalem he expects the name and praise of Yahweh to be proclaimed when the nations assemble there for worship (vv. 21–22; cf. v. 15). Though the things created by Yahweh are transitory (v. 26; cf. v. 11), the power of Yahweh himself, by contrast, will endure for years without end. This guarantees that the psalmist's descendants will be established in Yahweh's presence for generation after generation (v. 28; cf. v. 18).

Two themes in this psalm seem worthy of special comment. Here we find the first positive word about the nations in the Exile, a theme which will take on larger proportions in the books of Jeremiah, Ezekiel, and Second Isaiah. Secondly, the psalmist, burdened down with what we might call private trou-

19. The principal reason for assigning this psalm to the Exile is the reference to the rebuilding of Zion in vv. 13 and 16.

bles, sees his own future against the backdrop of Jerusalem's restoration. His future, therefore, is not just that of an isolated individual. The *nation's* hope means comfort for him as well.

CONCLUSION

Our study of Israel's exilic laments has shown not only how deep and painful the fall of Jerusalem was, but it has also uncovered the great variety of traditions about Yahweh that gave Jerusalemites courage and confidence in their prayers. If Hans Walter Wolff's understanding of Obadiah is correct, we can speak now also of the "other half" of lament worship in exile, in which prophetic oracles against Edom assured Israel that its complaints had been heard.[20] Interestingly enough, this prophetic assurance of salvation was grounded in the kingship of Yahweh (Obad. 21), to which the lamenting worshipers themselves had appealed in Lam. 5:19; Pss. 44:4; 74:10–17; and 102:12.

The laments are too short to develop detailed responses to exile, too emotionally involved with the events to give the required perspective, and frequently marked with accusations against Yahweh for unfairly handing Israel over to its enemies, being unable to help, being silent, forgetful, absent, or unreal. For the authors of the laments Yahweh had become an enemy.

It was left to succeeding theologians (e.g. the Deuteronomists) to meet these accusations by justifying God's actions in 587 as a legitimate response to Israel's sin. Thus those who had accused God in the laments became accused by him, a predicament from which they could only be delivered by God's forgiveness. It also was the task of succeeding exilic theologians (e.g. the exilic prophets and P) to announce God's acquitting word. Theirs was also the happy task of spelling out, with ever greater detail, just what the future after exile would look like—as we shall see.

20. Hans Walter Wolff, *Dodekapropheton 3: Obadja und Jona,* BKAT 14/3 (Neukirchen-Vluyn: Neukirchener Verlag, 1977). Cf. Lam. 4:21–23.

CHAPTER 2

The Secret Things

and the Things Revealed

Reactions to the Exile in the
Deuteronomistic History

The Deuteronomistic History (Dtr) is the name given to the Books of Deuteronomy, Joshua, Judges, 1 and 2 Samuel, and 1 and 2 Kings. The classic description of this work was made by Martin Noth in 1943.[1] Noth proposed that the Deuteronomistic historian (DtrH) composed his work in Palestine about the middle of the sixth century B.C., using numerous old traditions or sources. DtrH interpreted the history of Israel from the conquest to the fall of the southern kingdom on the basis of Deuteronomic theology. For this historian the tragic end of the people Israel was the fully justified and unavoidable consequence of their rejection of Yahweh during their entire stay in Palestine. Dtr, therefore, was a kind of confession of Israel's sin. Its purpose was overwhelmingly didactic and theological; the author was not trying to present an objective narrative of the facts of history.

DtrH's analyses of Israel's history are scattered throughout the work in specially composed speeches or prayers put into the mouths of leading figures (Moses, Deut. 1–3 [4], cf. 29–31; Joshua, Josh. 1 and 23; Samuel, 1 Sam. 12; and Solomon, 1 Kings 8). At times DtrH presented his analysis without putting it into an-

1. Martin Noth, *Überlieferungsgeschichtliche Studien* I, 3d ed. (Halle [Saale]: M. Niemeyer, 1967). Subsequent research has been analyzed, with extensive bibliographic references, by Arnold Nicolaas Radjawane, "Das deuteronomistische Geschichtswerk," *TRu* 38 (1974): 177–216.

23

other's mouth (Josh. 12; Judg. 2:11ff.; 2 Kings 17:7ff.). In recent years the oracle of Nathan and David's prayer in response to it, both in 2 Samuel 7, have also been viewed as examples of these interpretive keys.[2]

Whatever the redactional history of Dtr (preexilic and exilic editions[3] or a series of exilic redactions),[4] it seems to have achieved a nearly final form during the Exile. Dennis McCarthy has recently suggested that the final form of Dtr be interpreted as a rhetorical whole, as a unified structure of effective verbal expression. He notes that the essential meaning of a text grows out of its structure as a present (synchronic) whole.[5] Our question then in this chapter is, What does a reading of this final form of Dtr offer to exilic theology?

ACCOUNTING FOR ISRAEL'S EXILE IN THE TIME OF MOSES

Although the speaker in the parts of Deuteronomy assigned to Dtr is alleged to be Moses, the exilic author has left behind numerous clues that the real audience and the real time of composition are in the sixth century. In chap. 29, for example, reference is made to a coming generation that will experience afflictions and sicknesses and ask Yahweh why he has done this (vv. 22 and 24), but the writer is surely speaking about the circumstances of his own day, not about those of a future generation

2. See Frank M. Cross, *Canaanite Myth and Hebrew Epic* (Cambridge, Mass.: Harvard University Press, 1973), pp. 274–89, especially p. 275; and Dennis J. McCarthy, "II Samuel 7 and the Structure of the Deuteronomic History," *JBL* 84 (1965) : 131–38.

3. Cross, *Canaanite Myth*, pp. 284, 287–88.

4. Rudolf Smend, "Das Gesetz und die Völker, Ein Beitrag zur deuteronomistischen Redaktionsgeschichte," in *Probleme Biblischer Theologie*, ed. Hans Walter Wolff (Munich: Christian Kaiser, 1971), pp. 494–509; idem, *Die Entstehung des Alten Testaments* (Stuttgart: Kohlhammer, 1978), pp. 110–25; Walter Dietrich, *Prophetie und Geschichte, Eine redaktionsgeschichtliche Untersuchung zum deuteronomistischen Geschichtswerk*, FRLANT 108 (Göttingen: Vandenhoeck & Ruprecht, 1972) ; Timo Veijola, *Die ewige Dynastie: David und die Entstehung seiner Dynastie nach der deuteronomistischen Darstellung* (Helsinki: Suomalainen Tiedeakatemia, 1975) ; idem, *Das Königtum in der Beurteilung der deuteronomistischen Historiographie* (Helsinki: Suomalainen Tiedeakatemia, 1977).

5. Dennis McCarthy, "The Wrath of Yahweh and the Structural Unity of the Deuteronomistic History," *Essays in Old Testament Ethics*, ed. J. L. Crenshaw and J. T. Willis (New York: KTAV, 1974) , p. 99.

(cf. vv. 14–15, 27). The writer knew firsthand what exile meant.

Why has Yahweh destroyed his land (v. 24)?[6] DtrH answers his own question: because "they" forsook the covenant of Yahweh, the God of their fathers, and served other gods (vv. 25–26). Elsewhere he speaks of frustrating (*prr* Hiphil), transgressing (*'br*), not keeping (*l' šmr*), rejecting (*m's*), or forgetting (*škḥ*) the covenant.[7] The verbs are interchangeable synonyms; the real offense is the serving of other gods.[8] The result of these transgressions is an outbreak of God's anger and wrath (Deut. 29:20, 24, 27, 28; cf. 2 Kings 24:3, 20), his refusal to forgive (v. 20; cf. 2 Kings 24:4), and an unleashing of the curses of the covenant (vv. 20 and 27) recorded in Deuteronomy 28.

"Moses'" message for the exilic generation gains special poignancy and theological power precisely because it is delivered to Israel while it is on the verge of the land. Israel really received two gifts at that time: the land and the law. Both law and land are gifts of the promising and fulfilling God whose name is Yahweh.

Moses extends the land promise in Dtr by commanding Joshua to conquer and divide the land (Deut. 31:7; cf. Josh. 1:6), and his commands are executed to a T by Joshua. In Joshua 2—12 the Israelites carry out a lightning-quick takeover of Palestine, and Dtr concludes, "So Joshua took the whole land, according to all that Yahweh had spoken to Moses" (Josh. 11:23). Or even more exuberantly, "Not one of all the good promises which Yahweh had made to the house of Israel had failed; all came to pass" (Josh. 21:45).

In addition to this promise with its fulfillment, however, Dtr cites another word of Yahweh, foretelling that because the people would serve other gods and break the covenant, Yahweh would be angry and forsake them (Deut. 31:16–17, 20). This word not only explains the disaster of 587 as the result of the broken

---

6. Note the similar question in 1 Kings 9:8. The answer in 1 Kings 9:9 is similar to Deut. 29:25–26. Cf. also Jer. 5:19; 9:11–15; 16:10–13; 22:8–9.

7. For the references see Lothar Perlitt, *Bundestheologie im Alten Testament*, WMANT 36 (Neukirchen-Vluyn: Neukirchener Verlag, 1969), p. 36, n. 1.

8. Dtr describes the service of these gods in rows of verbs consisting of various combinations of "go after," "bow down to," "turn to," "fear," or "sacrifice to." For references see ibid., p. 36, n. 2.

covenant (cf. chap. 29), but it also makes that event a *consequence* of God's reliable word. Whereas Yahweh had proven faithful to the land promise and to his word that foretold Israel's fate, Israel had not kept the covenant at all despite the commands of Yahweh (Deut. 4:13, 14) and the warnings of Moses (Deut. 4:23–24). Failure to do what is right in Yahweh's eyes, Moses thundered, would lead to the loss of the land (4:26) and to a scattering among the nations (4:27). Despite such warnings, according to Dtr, north Israel went into Assyrian exile, because they "transgressed his covenant, even all that Moses the servant of Yahweh commanded" (2 Kings 18:12). This falling away began as soon as the conquest was completed. Immediately after Joshua's distribution of the land (Judg. 2:6), that is, precisely when the promise to the fathers had been dramatically fulfilled, DtrH reports, "The anger of Yahweh was kindled against Israel; and he said, 'Because this people have transgressed my covenant . . .' " (Judg. 2:20).

Thus from the beginning of Israel's history in the land until its end, the people's behavior could be characterized as a non-fulfilling of the covenant. And over against this infidelity stands the promising and fulfilling Yahweh, who added the gift of the law to the gift of the land and who had even announced with tragic accuracy on the verge of the land, "They will break my covenant" (Deut. 31:20).

With the loss of its land, exilic Israel could have been tempted to say, "Since we have lost the land, Yahweh, the one who promised the land, has become unreliable and untrustworthy." DtrH insists however on the unfailing connection between God's promise and its fulfillment. Israel's fate therefore stems from her own guilt, her unfaithfulness, her failure to keep the covenant—from the first to the last.

ACCOUNTING FOR ISRAEL'S EXILE IN THE TIME OF JOSHUA AND THE JUDGES

During the lifetime of Joshua all the promises about the land and its distribution were perfectly fulfilled (Josh. 21:43–45). Before his death, according to Dtr, Joshua assembled the people and rehearsed for them the great events of the conquest (23:3–5 and/or 24:8–13).[9] He urged them to avoid the worship of other gods (23:16; 24:14, 20, 23). Joshua's lifetime was a time of completely faithful Yahweh worship (Josh. 24:31 and Judg. 2:7).

For the period of the judges DtrH redacted a previously existing "Book of Saviors" (Retterbuch)[10] in order to make it contribute to his analysis of Israel's history. The Book of Saviors had structured the period of the judges in a repetitive pattern: Israel sinned, was handed over to an enemy, and cried to Yahweh. Then Yahweh raised up a saving hero, the enemy was subdued, and the land again had rest. DtrH inserted interpretive passages in 2:6— 3:6 and 10:6–16 and more minor additions elsewhere. He thereby made clear that the sin in the period of the judges was precisely that against which Joshua—and Moses—had warned, and which was to be the downfall of the northern and southern kingdoms, namely, the worship of other gods (2:12–13; 10:6, 10, 13–14). Such idolatrous worship inevitably called forth the wrath of Yahweh (2:14, 20; 10:7). He expanded the Retterbuch's cry to Yahweh in chap. 10 by turning it into an appropriate confession of sin: "And the people of Israel cried to Yahweh, saying, 'We have sinned against thee, because we have forsaken our God and have served the Baals'" (v. 10; cf. 1 Sam. 12:10).

DtrH indicated that the sin-punishment-deliverance cycle would not go on forever. Yahweh once refused to deliver Israel in the time of the judges (10:13) and was moved to act only when the people's confession was followed by an actual removal of the foreign gods (10:16). Only then, DtrH observes, did God become indignant over the misery of Israel.[11]

9. Noth, Überlieferungsgeschichtliche Studien, pp. 5 and 9, held chap. 23 to be original in Dtr and 24 to be a secondary addition; Smend, "Das Gesetz und die Völker," p. 501, holds the opposite to be true. In any case, Dtr always seems to have contained at least one of these speeches.

10. See the thorough analysis of Wolfgang Richter, Die Bearbeitungen des "Retterbuches" in der deuteronomischen Epoche, BBB 21 (Bonn: Peter Hanstein, 1964). Richter's book and some additional studies are conveniently summarized by I. Schlauri, "Wolfgang Richter's Beitrag zur Redaktionsgeschichte des Richterbuches," Bib 54 (1973): 367–403.

11. Similarly, Yahweh turned from his burning anger over Achan's stealing of the "devoted things" only when Israel had stoned the offender and buried him under a heap of stones, thus decisively rejecting his sin (Josh. 7:26; cf. Deut. 13:17–18).

DtrH further modified the *Retterbuch* in that he omitted its "rest formula" in his own interpretive insertions in chaps. 2 and 10. This means that the story of Jephthah in particular does not end in a period of rest, but the story moves on into the disturbed times of Samson, Samuel, and Saul. The addition of the word "again" (*wayyōsīpû*) to the sin formula (3:12; 4:1; 10:6; 13:1; cf. 8:33) pushes his interpretation another step farther. The sins of Israel consequently are not just a series of independent fallings-away from Yahweh, but they are continuous and indeed growing. The climax of Israel's sin in the period of the judges comes with the desire for a king (1 Sam. 12:19).[12] While the following verses provide forgiveness for the people, the kingship of Saul ("the king whom *you* have chosen," 1 Sam. 12:13) is never really accepted in Dtr. In chap. 13 Samuel delivers an emphatic rejection of Saul and his kingship (vv. 13–15).

Israel sinned in the period of the judges by choosing other gods and by demanding a king like the nations. It did this in spite of God's total keeping of the land promise; in fact, it did this as soon as the land promise had been fulfilled (cf. Judg. 2:6). Even during this period Israel did not lack new evidences of God's goodness. DtrH notes that the judges were raised up by God and accompanied by him through all their days (2:18). Israel's salvation did not come merely from the heroic acts of ancient saviors. Rather, "He [that is, Yahweh] saved them from the hand of their enemies" (2:18).

The nature of the people's sin in this period is specified by a series of passages that find Israel's guilt in the transgression of the law of Moses and in its mixing with the nations and the following of their gods (Josh. 1:7–9; 13:1b–6; and chap. 23). In Judg. 2:20–21, 23 the people's service of the nations' gods led to an appropriate and ominous punishment. Yahweh ceased to expel the nations left after Joshua's initial battles (Josh. 23:4, 7, 12). Instead these nations—and their idolatrous temptations—were left as a snare, a trap, a scourge, and thorns in the people's eyes until Israel perished from the good land (Josh. 23:13).

This motif serves at least two functions: (*a*) It wards off any

---

12. Cf. 1 Sam. 8:7, where Yahweh says that in asking for a king the people have not rejected Samuel but Yahweh himself.

attempt by Israel to excuse its idolatrous actions by blaming them on the non-Yahwistic nations in their land; Israel's own sins in its early days were responsible for the presence of these deadly tempters. Secondly, (*b*) it warned the remnant left in Palestine after 587 not to become involved in syncretistic alliances with other peoples in the land, following the pattern of north Israel after 721 (cf. 2 Kings 17:24–40). The threats in Josh. 23:13 and 16 may mean that Yahweh could wipe even the survivors of 587 off the land.

ACCOUNTING FOR ISRAEL'S EXILE IN THE TIME OF THE MONARCHY

The United Monarchy

The first kingship under Saul is judged negatively in Dtr because it arose from the people's own choice (cf. 1 Sam. 12:19) and because of the behavior of Saul himself. Despite Israel's sin in choosing Saul, Yahweh would have established a dynasty for him, according to Dtr, but Saul erred in performing a sacrifice in the place of Samuel (1 Sam. 13:8–14) and in not carrying out the ban in a war against Amalek (1 Sam. 15).

Saul serves as a foil to David, whom God chose, and whose behavior was considered perfect by DtrH. God's choice of David as king of Israel instead of Saul, his dynastic promise to him, and his care for him are frequently attested (by Samuel, 1 Sam. 13: 13–14 and 28:17; by Jonathan, 1 Sam. 20:15 and 23:17; by Saul, 1 Sam. 24:20–21; by Abigail, 1 Sam. 25:28, 30; by Abner, 2 Sam. 3:9–10, 18; by the tribes of Israel, 2 Sam. 5:1–2; and by David himself, 2 Sam. 6:21; cf. 5:12). But it is in 2 Samuel 7 that the promise to David receives its most thorough expression, both in the oracle of Nathan (vv. 8–17) and in David's prayer (vv. 18–29). Six times we are told that David's kingship, his house, or his throne will last forever (vv. 13, 16, 25, 29). This unconditional promise to David required correction by DtrH to explain Jerusalem's eventual fall, but it also offered some hope as the historian turned toward the future.

Dtr presents David as a perfect man in spite of the murder and adultery ascribed to him in the pre-Deuteronomistic sources. Only

Moses, Joshua, and David are designated as Yahweh's servants in Dtr. David stands out because he captured Jerusalem and cared for the ark (2 Sam. 5 and 6), and because of his prayers (2 Sam. 7:18–29 and 1 Kings 1:47–48). Though his plan to build a temple was postponed to the time of his son because of his wars (1 Kings 5:3–5), his pious intention is given full praise (1 Kings 8:17–19). We are told that David administered justice and equity to all the people (2 Sam. 8:15), walked before Yahweh in faithfulness, in righteousness, and in uprightness of heart (1 Kings 3:6) and in Yahweh's ways (1 Kings 11:33), and kept Yahweh's statutes and commandments (1 Kings 3:14). His heart was "wholly true to Yahweh" (1 Kings 15:3), and he did what was right in the eyes of Yahweh and did not turn aside from anything that he commanded him all the days of his life (1 Kings 15:5).[13]

Because of the promises to David and because of David's perfect obedience (cf. 2 Sam. 22:22–25), Yahweh postponed the punishment merited by later kings, or he did not fully carry it out. The division of the kingdom, accordingly, did not take place in Solomon's lifetime because of David (1 Kings 11:12; cf. v. 32), and the southern dynasty retained one tribe even after the split because of God's choice of David and Jerusalem (1 Kings 11:13, 32, 36). Yahweh gave Abijam dominion (a lamp) in Jerusalem because David did what was right (1 Kings 15:4), and the promise of dominion to David forestalled total destruction during the reign of wicked Jehoram (2 Kings 8:19). Yahweh's choice of David and Jerusalem also led to his defense of the city during the days of Hezekiah (2 Kings 19:39; 20:6).

This idealized picture of David serves too as a model for evaluating succeeding kings. So the wicked behavior of Solomon (1 Kings 11:4, 6, 33), Jeroboam I (1 Kings 14:8; cf. 11:38), Abijam (1 Kings 15:30), and Ahaz (2 Kings 16:2) stands in bold and explicit contrast to that of David. Even a good king like Amaziah (2 Kings 14:3) did not fully live up to the standards of David his father. Only Asa (1 Kings 5:11) and the great reformers, Hezekiah and Josiah, are held to be his equal (2 Kings 18:3 and 22:2).

---

13. Apparently this was too much for a later redactor who added the words "except in the matter of Uriah the Hittite," but this phrase is lacking in the LXX and surely secondary.

In Dtr's account of David's son, Solomon, we find much about his role as temple builder. He built the house for Yahweh's name in exact fulfillment of the promise to David (2 Sam. 7:13; 1 Kings 5:5; 8:20). But two other factors are also of great importance in the Solomon accounts. First, Dtr here makes the promise to David conditional, that is, the Davidic dynasty will be permanent only if the sons of David walk before Yahweh in faithfulness, with all their heart and with all their soul (1 Kings 2:3–4; 8:25; 9:4–5; cf. 6:12–13). This addition made clear why, despite the great promises to David, Yahweh was justified in sending the terrible events of 587. Secondly, DtrH begins his accounting of royal unfaithfulness with Solomon. We are told in 1 Kings 11:4–8, 33 that Solomon's wives turned away his heart after other gods when he was old (cf. Deut. 7:4). Solomon also went after Ashtoreth of the Sidonians, Milcom of the Ammonites, and Chemosh of the Moabites, and built high places for these gods in the vicinity of Jerusalem (cf. 2 Kings 23:13). Solomon's (cf. *BHS*) forsaking of Yahweh and worship of other gods had the division of the kingdom as its ultimate consequence (1 Kings 11:33). Each kingdom henceforth had its special sins and its special history of judgment.

North Israel

DtrH accounts for the fall of the northern kingdom primarily by his comments on Jeroboam and the dynasty of Omri and by his concluding summary in 2 Kings 17:7ff.

Jeroboam's sins consisted in his erecting sanctuaries at Bethel and Dan (1 Kings 12:30; 13:34). Whatever Jeroboam's own intentions were, DtrH viewed these sanctuaries as violations of the law of the single sanctuary (e.g. Deut. 12) and as centers of idolatry (1 Kings 12:28). By this evil Jeroboam threw away a chance to have as sure a dynasty as David's (1 Kings 11:38). High places and Asherim existed in Jeroboam's time (1 Kings 12:31, 32; 13:2, 32–33; 14:15), and his sins led the whole people Israel to sin (1 Kings 14:16).[14]

Just as David was the standard of comparison in the south, so

14. Almost all the succeeding kings are said to have caused Israel to sin (Shallum and Hoshea are the only exceptions). In the south only Manasseh "caused Judah to sin."

Jeroboam played this role in the north, though his was a completely negative example. His son, Nadab, continued in the sin
of Jeroboam (1 Kings 15:26), as did Baasha, the founder of the
next dynasty (1 Kings 15:34; 16:2; cf. 16:12), and Zimri of the
third northern house (1 Kings 16:19). Omri, Ahab, and Ahaziah
had their own grievous faults, but Dtr reports that they also
walked in the way of Jeroboam (1 Kings 16:25–26, 30; 22:52–53).
Ten of the final twelve kings are judged in a stereotyped formula
that adds no new information: "He also did evil in the eyes of
Yahweh; he did not depart from all the sins of Jeroboam the son
of Nebat, which he made Israel to sin."[15] The Jeroboam theme
receives its final statement in 2 Kings 17:21–22, where both king
and people are made to share in guilt.[16]

Omri was surely one of the most important kings in north
Israel's history. He founded the new capital at Samaria, and
Israel was known in Assyrian records as the house of Omri even
after his dynasty was overthrown. Yet Dtr treats him in a scant
thirteen verses (1 Kings 16:16–28) and notes laconically that he
did more evil than all who were before him (1 Kings 16:25). Dtr
pauses at length, however, over Omri's son Ahab (1 Kings 16:28—
22:40). He too did evil in the sight of Yahweh more than all who
were before him (1 Kings 16:30; cf. v. 33). Not only did he follow
all the sins of Jeroboam, but he married a Tyrian princess,
Jezebel, who brought four hundred fifty prophets of Baal and
four hundred prophets of Asherah to eat at her table (1 Kings
18:19), and he built a temple for Baal in Samaria (1 Kings 16:32).
His struggles with the prophet Elijah were epic, and the issues
involved included Yahweh's claims over against Baal's (cf. the
scene at Mt. Carmel, 1 Kings 18) and the sanctity of land tenure
by private citizens (cf. Naboth's vineyard, 1 Kings 21). Ahab's
oldest son, Ahaziah, scarcely fared better in Dtr. He walked in the
way of his father, and in the way of his mother, and in the way

---

15. Cf. 2 Kings 3:2–3; 10:29; 13:2, 11; 14:24; 15:9, 18, 24, 28. See the "Tabelle
zum Schema 1N" in Helga Weippert, "Die 'deuteronomistischen' Beurtei-
lungen der Könige von Israel und Juda und das Problem der Redaktion der
Königsbücher," *Bib* 53 (1972) : 309.

16. In the passages listed in n. 15 we are told only that the king himself did
not depart from these sins. Though DtrH judged the nation by its kings, he
also asserts that the people shared in this guilt. Cf. 2 Kings 13:6.

of Jeroboam. He provoked Yahweh to anger in every way that his father had done (1 Kings 22:52–53). Interestingly, the phrase "provoke to anger" is only used in the north for the kings from Jeroboam to Ahaziah—by the time the history of these kings has been told, DtrH has fully necessitated the fall of Samaria. Ahaziah's brother, Jehoram, who succeeded him on the throne, did evil too, though not like his father and mother (2 Kings 3:2). DtrH tells us that he actually removed the pillar of Baal which his father had made. From Jehoram on Dtr dismisses the remaining kings as mere copies of Jeroboam the son of Nebat.

The road from Jeroboam's sin to the defeat of 721 is almost straight downhill in Dtr, but small acts of piety are able to effect delays, as did David's election and piety in the south. Because Ahab repented after Elijah's blistering word of judgment in the Naboth incident, the end of his dynasty was postponed to the era of his sons (1 Kings 21:27–29). Jehu did not turn aside from the sins of Jeroboam (2 Kings 10:29), but he did execute God's judgment on Joram, the last of Ahab's sons to reign in the north (2 Kings 9:24), and on Ahaziah in the south, "who walked in the ways of the house of Ahab" (2 Kings 8:22 and 9:27). Moreover, he executed Jezebel in fulfillment of the word of Yahweh (2 Kings 9:36; cf. 1 Kings 21:23). Whatever *we* think of Jehu's slaughter of Ahab's seventy sons, the kinsmen of Ahaziah, the remnant of Ahab in Samaria, and the worshipers of Baal (2 Kings 10:1–25), DtrH himself clearly approves Jehu's burning of Baal's pillar and his turning the temple of Baal into a latrine (2 Kings 10:26–27). Jehu wiped out Baal from Israel (2 Kings 10:28)! Despite Jehu's maintenance of the calves of Bethel and Dan, his line was extended for four more generations (2 Kings 10:30), making his the longest dynasty in north Israel's history (cf. 2 Kings 13:4–6, 23; 14:26–27; and 15:12).

But with Jeroboam and Ahab things had already gone too far, and at least ten of the last twelve kings of the north are said to have merely repeated Jeroboam's mistakes. No particular guilt is attributed to Hoshea, the last king; he was not even considered as evil as the kings who were before him (2 Kings 17:2). His infidelity to his Assyrian suzerain, to be sure, was the proximate cause of Assyria's final attack (2 Kings 17:3–6), but the ultimate cause was the people's sins against Yahweh (v. 7). In his final, sermonic summation DtrH documents how the people had feared other gods. They had been just like the nations despite the explicit command of God and his repeated warnings through the prophets. The people repeated the sins of their fathers and participated in all kinds of idolatry. They, like the kings from Jeroboam to Ahaziah, aye, like their fathers in the days of Moses (Deut. 29:20, 24, 27, 28) and in the days of the judges (Judg. 2:14, 20; 3:8), had provoked Yahweh to anger (2 Kings 17:7–17).

Now Yahweh's anger knew no constraint; he removed them out of his presence in fulfillment of his word via the prophets (2 Kings 17:18, 23). The sum of this history is fully right to DtrH: "Israel was exiled from their own land to Assyria until this day" (2 Kings 17:23).

The Southern Kingdom

Dtr's accounting for the fall of the southern kingdom can be sampled in his discussion of the time of Rehoboam, the first king in the south, and of the time of Manasseh, one of the last southern kings.

Rehoboam[17] did what was evil in the sight of Yahweh and provoked Yahweh to jealousy more than his fathers had done by all their sins (1 Kings 14:22). The crucial role of this paragraph on Rehoboam is shown by the mention of his provoking Yahweh to jealousy (qn' Piel). DtrH uses another term for provocation (k's Hiphil) in his discussion of Manasseh (2 Kings 21:6; 23:26) and of the sins of the people at his time (2 Kings 21:16), as well as in the climactic oracle of Huldah, where the people's worship of other gods is said to be the provocation for God's unquenchable wrath (2 Kings 22:17).

Rehoboam did "more" provocations than his fathers. We have seen this "more than" comparison used for Omri and Ahab in the north,[18] and it is used also for Manasseh: he did things "more evil" than the Amorites (2 Kings 21:11), the pre-Israelite inhabi-

17. So LXX; cf. *BHS.*
18. Each generation in the period of the judges also behaved worse than their fathers (Judg. 2:19).

tants of Palestine. Manasseh, in fact, seduced the people "to do more evil than the nations had done whom Yahweh destroyed before the people of Israel" (2 Kings 21:9; cf. v. 2 and 1 Kings 14:24; 2 Kings 16:3; 17:8, 11, 15).

The people at Rehoboam's time sinned by building high places (1 Kings 14:23). Whatever the actual function of these sanctuaries had been in Israel, for DtrH they are clearly idolatrous (cf. Deut. 12:2–3 and 1 Kings 12:31–32). Manasseh later rebuilt the high places (2 Kings 21:3) after Hezekiah had torn them down, only to have Josiah abolish them once and for all in his great reform (2 Kings 23:5–20). Outside of these notices at the beginning and end of the southern kingdom, DtrH cites the high places only in a cliché qualifying his good evaluation of five kings (Jehoshaphat, Joash, Amaziah, Azariah, and Jotham): "yet they did not take away the high places,[19] and the people sacrificed and burned incense on the high places." We note that DtrH does not limit his condemnation here to the kings; from the very start of the southern kingdom, and repeatedly throughout its history, the people matched the kings in apostasy. The people set up pillars in Rehoboam's day (1 Kings 14:23; cf. 2 Kings 18:4 and 23:14) and erected Asherim (1 Kings 14:23; cf. Asa's mother, 1 Kings 15:13, and Manasseh, 2 Kings 21:3, 7). The emergence of cult prostitutes in Rehoboam's days (1 Kings 14:24) was directly contrary to Deuteronomic law (Deut. 23:18), though its abiding power among the people is attested by Dtr in the accounts of Asa's (1 Kings 15:12), Jehoshaphat's (1 Kings 22:46), and Josiah's (2 Kings 23:7) attempts to eradicate it.

The paragraphs above have already indicated how frequently the sins of Rehoboam's days were repeated by Manasseh, and these references need not be repeated here. What makes Manasseh worse in DtrH's eyes is that he restored these idolatrous practices after Hezekiah's reform. Moreover, he erected an altar for Baal and Asherah as Ahab, king of Israel, had done (2 Kings 21: 3). Such comparison with the northern kings is a frequent part of DtrH's polemic. Not only does he castigate the southern kings

---

19. Translation RWK. This first half of the formula is also used of Asa.

Jehoram and Ahaziah for walking in the way of the house of Ahab (2 Kings 8:18, 27), but he scores the southerner Ahaz for performing child sacrifice as he walked in the ways of the kings of north Israel (2 Kings 16:3; cf. 2 Kings 21:6).

Because of all Manasseh's sins itemized above and more,[20] and because he made Judah to sin with his idols (2 Kings 21:11), Yahweh announced through his prophets: "I will stretch over Jerusalem the measuring line of Samaria, and the plummet of the house of Ahab; and I will wipe Jerusalem as one wipes a dish, wiping it and turning it upside down. And I will cast off the remnant of my heritage" (2 Kings 21:13–14; cf. 23:26–27; 24:3–4).

The final blow came later in Judah than in Israel. This delay resulted in part from God's choice of David and his promise to give him dominion in Jerusalem; partly, this resulted from David's own behavior. Partly, it came from the merits of the three kings discussed below of whom DtrH reported, "They did what was right in Yahweh's eyes like David their father." Such behavior was the necessary prerequisite if Yahweh were to establish David's royal throne over Israel forever (1 Kings 2:4; 8:25; 9:4–5).

Asa showed David-like piety by ridding the land of cult prostitutes and removing all the idols his fathers had made. He deposed the idol-worshiping queen mother and burned her Asherah. His heart was wholly true to Yahweh all his days (1 Kings 15:11–14).

Hezekiah, too, followed David in all things. He sacked the high places, pillars, and Asherah; he even destroyed the bronze serpent Nehushtan, before which Israel burned incense (cf. Num. 21:6–9). His trust in Yahweh was without equal among the kings of Judah, and he kept all the commandments of Moses. Not surprisingly he gained a series of military victories (2 Kings 18:1–8; cf. 1 Kings 15:16–22).

No one was more like David, however, than Josiah: he did not

---

20. He worshiped the host of heaven, constructed altars for them in the temple, practiced soothsaying and augury, used mediums and wizards, and shed innocent blood (2 Kings 21:3–5, 16; cf. 2 Kings 24:4). Amon, Manasseh's son, was just as evil as his father (2 Kings 21:19–26).

turn aside to the right hand or to the left (2 Kings 22:2). His every action was designed to implement the provisions of the book of the law (= Deuteronomy) found in the temple (2 Kings 22:8–13). He and the people made a covenant to keep Yahweh's commandments. He cleansed the temple of all paraphernalia of Baal, Asherah, and the host of heaven, destroyed the high places, broke down the houses of the cult prostitutes, wrecked the child sacrifice installations in Hinnom, and pulled down the altar at Bethel. He celebrated a Passover just like it had been celebrated in the days of the judges (2 Kings 23:1–23). In sum: "Before him there was no king like him, who turned to Yahweh with all his heart and with all his soul and with all his might, according to all the law of Moses" (2 Kings 23:25).

Still, after Manasseh, even a Josiah could no longer stem the tide of judgment (2 Kings 23:26–27; 24:3–4). DtrH records two oracles of Huldah, to whom the book of the law found in the temple was taken. In the first (2 Kings 22:16–17), Huldah announced that all the curses found in the book (presumably an early form of Deut. 28) would come on Jerusalem, because the people had forsaken Yahweh and burned incense to other gods to provoke Yahweh to unquenchable wrath. In the second (2 Kings 22:18–20), Huldah promised the king a peaceful end. By putting the two oracles side by side and by dutifully reporting Josiah's tragic death at the hands of Neco (2 Kings 23:28–30), DtrH indicates that the king's exemplary behavior was only able to benefit himself; it was not able to save the people. Presumably, the second oracle of Huldah in its Dtr context is understood to mean that Josiah would die prior to the dread events of 597 and 587, and hence he died "in peace."[21]

In his description of the sins of Manasseh and his predecessors, DtrH had fully justified the events of 587. The last four southern kings are referred to almost in passing. Each did what was evil in the eyes of Yahweh either (*a*) according to all which his fathers had done (Jehoahaz and Jehoiakim) or (*b*) according to all which

---

21. For the devastating effect of Josiah's death on Hebrew historiography, see Stanley Brice Frost, "The Death of Josiah: A Conspiracy of Silence," *JBL* 87 (1968) : 369–82.

Jehoiakim did (Jehoiachin and Zedekiah). Dtr's bottom line on the south echoes his treatment of the north: "So Judah was taken into exile out of its land" (2 Kings 25:21; cf. 17:23).

ANTICIPATING THE FUTURE IN DTR

According to Martin Noth, DtrH intended to show only that God's punishment was justified.[22] From conquest to 587, God had accompanied the ever increasing apostasy with warnings and punishments. When these proved fruitless, he sent complete destruction. Dtr, in Noth's view, explained the past history but promised nothing for the future. We read in Deut. 29:29, "The secret things belong to Yahweh our God; but the things that are revealed belong to us and our children for ever, that we may do all the works of this law." What has been revealed is the Decalogue and its official explication in Deuteronomy. Doing this law should be the preoccupation of Israel. But the future is veiled, hidden, unrevealed—hence DtrH's reticence to speak about it. But is Noth right that the book has only a pessimistic, backward-looking aim?

THE PROMISE TO THE FATHERS

Dtr makes frequent references to the oath Yahweh made to the fathers to give them the land (Deut. 1:8, 35, etc.). When Yahweh established Israel as his people and became their God, he was keeping the promise made to Abraham, Isaac, and Jacob (Deut. 29:13). That promise to the fathers formed the basis for God's mercy when north Israel underwent severe oppression by the Arameans: "Yahweh was gracious to them and had compassion on them, and he turned toward them, because of his covenant with Abraham, Isaac, and Jacob" (2 Kings 13:23). This promise to the fathers also provided hope for a return to Yahweh in present and future times of trouble: "For Yahweh your God is a merciful God; he will not fail you or destroy you or forget the

---

22. Noth, *Überlieferungsgeschichtliche Studien*, p. 100. Cf. also idem, "Zur Geschichtsauffassung des Deuteronomisten," in *Proceedings of the Twenty-Second Congress of Orientalists Held in Istanbul, 1951* (Leiden: E. J. Brill, 1957) 2: 558–66.

covenant with your fathers which he swore to them" (Deut. 4:31). One strong ray of hope in Dtr, then, stems from God's oath or promise, yes, his covenant with the Patriarchs.

THE PROMISE TO DAVID

Gerhard von Rad suggested that two words of Yahweh permeated Dtr. On the one hand there was the word of Moses and the prophets, whose laws and threats were ignored, leading to the events of 721 and 587. But on the other hand there was the promise to David in 2 Samuel 7 that led to reprieves for Judah's kings and that had had a recent fulfillment, that was itself full of hope and promise, in the release of Jehoiachin from prison.[23] Von Rad called attention to the numerous prophetic words of Yahweh which received explicit fulfillment in Dtr (e.g. 1 Kings 11:29ff. in 12:15), and he interpreted the promise to David in 2 Samuel 7 as one of these creative words of Yahweh active in history. Hans Walter Wolff criticized Von Rad's thesis, arguing that the promise in 2 Samuel 7 was always conditioned in Dtr (cf. 1 Kings 2:3–4 and 9:5–6; cf. Deut. 17:18–19) and that 2 Kings 25:27–30 makes no reference to the oracle of Nathan.[24]

Yet the issue is not yet settled. Von Rad may have erred in terming the Jehoiachin incident messianic and in making its promise virtually equivalent to the other, judgmental word. Veijola's recent study, however, has called renewed attention to the unconditional character of 2 Samuel 7 even in the final form of Dtr.[25] The repeated stress on the permanence of the Davidic house seems to be most appropriate precisely when this notion was under greatest suspicion, that is, during the Exile.

Erich Zenger has advanced the discussion by clarifying the structure of 2 Kings 25 and by explicating the significance of

23. Gerhard von Rad, *Studies in Deuteronomy* (London: SCM Press, 1953), chap. 7; idem, *Old Testament Theology* (New York: Harper & Row, Publishers, 1962) 1:334ff.
24. Hans Walter Wolff, "The Kerygma of the Deuteronomic Historical Work," *The Vitality of Old Testament Traditions* (Atlanta: John Knox Press, 1975), pp. 85–86.
25. Veijola, *Die ewige Dynastie*, pp. 68–79.

vv. 27–30 on the basis of Assyrian parallels.[26] According to the latter verses, Amel Marduk gave public and official recognition to the exiled king as a royal vassal. He summoned him to an audience, repeated the treaty between Babylon and Jehoiachin ("he spoke good with him," v. 28), and assigned him to a particularly high rank among the vassals. Jehoiachin received clothes appropriate to this new station and shared a meal with the king at the conclusion of the audience.[27] Finally, Jehoiachin was given ongoing financial support from the royal budget.

Second Kings 25:1–26, on the other hand, shows how Judah had reached an absolute nadir. Zedekiah was exiled in fetters to Babylon having witnessed the murder of his sons shortly before he was blinded. Nebuzaradan burned the temple and the palace and exiled some of the remaining populace, taking whatever was of value from the temple to Babylon. Top temple officials, various members of the royal administration, and sixty of the people of the land were then transported to Riblah—just like Zedekiah—where they were executed, perhaps as an example to the others. Judah was thus taken into exile out of its lands. Finally, Ishmael and his associates assassinated Gedaliah (cf. Jer. 40 and 41). As a result of this murder, the last remaining hope in Palestine was gone. When the remnant of the people fled to Egypt, they fulfilled, at least approximately, the final curse of Deuteronomy 28: "Yahweh will bring you back in ships (= as slaves) to Egypt" (v. 68).

After the depths of this end point had been noted, DtrH included the account of Jehoiachin's rehabilitation. In this event he may have seen the beginning of a new era of blessing, though it would be going much too far to call it messianic. No acts of deliverance are predicated of Jehoiachin. The secret things—the future—still belong to Yahweh (Deut. 29:29). By including both conditional (1 Kings 2:3–4; 9:5–6) and unconditional (2 Sam. 7) forms of the Davidic promise, DtrH was able to make room for the final humiliation of the Davidic line (in Zedekiah) and for a continuing positive effect of the promise to David (in Jehoiachin).

26. Erich Zenger, "Die deuteronomische Interpretation der Rehabilitierung Jojachins," *BZ* 12 (1968) : 16–30.
27. Zenger has argued convincingly that the words "every day of his life" and "regularly" in v. 29 are secondary additions from v. 30.

God is still acting for his people; his good word can still be trusted when the land is lost.

TURN[28]

Throughout the present form of Dtr, Israel is urged to turn or repent. Samuel urged turning and the removal of foreign gods at the time of the Philistine crisis (1 Sam. 7:3), and DtrH noted that every prophet urged repentance though their words fell on deaf ears (2 Kings 17:13). Sermons on repentance by Moses ring the core of Deuteronomy (4:29–31 and 30:1–10), and Solomon laced his prayer at the temple dedication with references to repentance at time of military defeat, drought, famine, and even exile (1 Kings 8:33–53). The cyclic history in the time of the judges proceeds from (a) sin to (b) punishment, but this is followed by (c) crying to Yahweh and then (d) deliverance. Dtr's history of the monarchy in a sense stops at the second stage of this cycle, perhaps implying that Israel's sin and punishment once more should be followed by a cry to Yahweh for help even now.[29] Josiah, who in so many ways is Dtr's ideal king, turned to Yahweh with all his heart, soul, and might; no king before him could match his example (2 Kings 23:25). In the following paragraphs we will discuss this repentance motif in three crucial passages that deal directly with the situation of exile, namely, two sermons of Moses and the prayer of Solomon.

The second sermon of Moses makes God's deliverance *conditional* upon Israel's repentance (Deut. 30:1–2, 9–10), but the first seems to *promise* that Israel will repent (Deut. 4:29–30). All three of our texts declare that such repentance will occur among those who are exiled from the land (Deut. 4:29; 30:1; 1 Kings 8:46–48).

Turning to Yahweh, according to Dtr, should happen wholeheartedly (Deut. 30:2; 1 Kings 8:48), and it is to be followed by

---

28. The significance of this motif has been explicated by Wolff, "The Kerygma," pp. 83–100. Wolff argues that Deut. 4:29–31 and 30:1–10 are late strata in Dtr, showing a relationship to parts of Jeremiah. Walter Brueggemann, "The Kerygma of the Deuteronomistic Historian," *Int* 22 (1968): 387–402, supplements Wolff's work by demonstrating how Dtr urged Israel to repent on the basis of Yahweh's continuing "goodness."
29. McCarthy, "The Wrath of Yahweh," p. 106.

listening to the voice of Yahweh (Deut. 4:30; 30:2, 8) and keeping all the commandments mediated by Moses (Deut. 30:8, 10).
Turning also should involve a confession of Israel's guilt (1 Kings
8:47). In other words, the recognition and acknowledgment of
the justice of God's actions in 721 and 587, which Noth made
the chief burden of Dtr's message, is really only one part of the
called-for repentance or turning. The year 587 is not a dead
end, just as God's refusal to deliver in the time of the judges was
not his last word (Judg. 10:13). Faced with God's "no" in those
early days, Israel confessed her sins and amended her life by
putting away the foreign gods (10:15-16), and—as a result—
Yahweh became indignant once more over the misery of Israel
(10:16). Solomon laid special stress on Israel's supplication to
Yahweh in time of distress as a part of her turning (1 Kings
8:47-49, 52; cf. vv. 33, 35, 38-39).

Israel is urged by Dtr to repent and to expect a positive response. God's character and past history with Israel both provide
adequate motivation for turning and justify positive expectations. Yahweh is a merciful God, who will not fail or destroy
Israel; he will not forget the covenant with the patriarchs even
in exile (Deut. 4:31). Armed with similar assurances (Deut. 31:6,
8), Joshua was equipped to begin the task of conquest.

Solomon—and therefore really DtrH—urged prayer toward
the land which Yahweh gave to the fathers, toward the city which
Yahweh had chosen, and to the house he built for his name.
Israel's own status as Yahweh's people was forged in the Exodus
from Egypt and communicated through Moses. Israel had been
selected from all the peoples of the earth (1 Kings 8:51-53).
These traditions of promise and election, or better, the God who
stands behind these promises, is a resource for hope, a refuge for
those banished to exile.

What will result from this turning? Repentant Israel can expect Yahweh to hear and do justice for them (1 Kings 8:49; cf.
8:45). Solomon, in addition, pleads with Yahweh to forgive them
(1 Kings 8:50; cf. vv. 34, 36, 39). To be sure, Yahweh had refused to forgive the sins of Manasseh (2 Kings 24:4; cf. Deut.
29:20) as he had refused at least temporarily to deliver Israel in
the time of the judges (Judg. 10:13). A repentant Israel can hope

for a different answer. Perhaps Yahweh will have compassion on such an Israel (Deut. 30:3) and will move their captor nations also to treat them with compassion (1 Kings 8:50).

In Deut. 30:1–10 DtrH goes farther than anywhere else in lifting the veil on the secret things of God's future. Israel's turning will be mirrored by Yahweh's turning (Deut. 30:3). Dtr seems to refer to a new exodus and a new gift of the land in vv. 3–5 (cf. 1 Kings 8:34). Yahweh's future goodness in fact will outstrip his kindness in the past. He will make Israel more prosperous and more numerous than their fathers (v. 5). His blessing will lead to fertility in man and beast, and to abundant crops (v. 9). He will circumcise their hearts (v. 6) so that they can love God with all their heart and soul. God will lift the richly deserved curses from Israel and will place them on their enemies (v. 7), a theme adumbrated at a number of points in Lamentations.

DtrH's urging of Israel to repent on the basis of God's character and past history with Israel, and his limited spelling out of God's response, must not be exaggerated. Some or most of these materials may not have been part of Dtr's original message, and even in the final redaction of Dtr they occupy a tiny portion of this rather lengthy historical work. The quantitative and emotional impact of the work centers on Israel's faithless response to Yahweh's many gifts, especially his gift of the land and the law.

The consequences of this infidelity in the defeats of 721 and 587 were wholly justified and should not have been unexpected— prophets and seers had warned Israel of God's onrushing judgment throughout its history. But however justified this word was, however devastating the effect of this wrath and of Yahweh's refusal to forgive, however much Yahweh was acquitted of all the charges against him, this word was not, finally, the last word of Yahweh, and 587 was not the end of Israel. The promise to the patriarchs still endured. Midway through the Exile God was still acting for Israel as exemplified by the rehabilitation of Jehoaichin. The task of the hour was for Israel, as part of her turning to Yahweh, to acknowledge God's justice, to listen to his voice, and to do his law. And then, though Dtr even in its final form is short on details, Israel could hope that Yahweh, in his unpredictable freedom, would act as Savior once more.

CHAPTER 3

Saying Yes to Exile—
and No!

*Reactions to the Exile in the
Book of Jeremiah*[1]

This chapter will distinguish between Jeremiah himself and the anonymous editor or editors who gave his message a new direction after the prophet had departed from the scene. My approach is that of redaction criticism rather than that of source criticism. I have been influenced very much, as the following pages show, by E. W. Nicholson[2] and especially by Winfried Thiel.[3]

Thiel believes that the Book of Jeremiah was given a Deuteronomistic redaction (hereafter often D) in Palestine around 550 B.C., which gave shape to virtually the entire book.[4] The redac-

1. For details see the commentaries of John Bright, *Jeremiah*, AB 21 (Garden City, NY: Doubleday, 1965), and Wilhelm Rudolph, *Jeremia*, HAT I, 123 (Tübingen: J. C. B. Mohr [Paul Siebeck], 1968). See also Siegfried Herrmann, *Die prophetischen Heilserwartungen im Alten Testament* BWANT 85 (Stuttgart: W. Kohlhammer, 1965), 159–241.
2. E. W. Nicholson, *Preaching to the Exiles: A Study of the Prose Tradition in the Book of Jeremiah* (New York: Schocken Books, 1971). See the review by Winfried Thiel in *TLZ* 97 (1972): 25–27.
3. Winfried Thiel, *Die deuteronomistische Redaktion von Jeremia 1—25*, WMANT 41 (Neukirchen-Vluyn: Neukirchener Verlag, 1973). Unfortunately, the second half of Thiel's dissertation, which was available to me in typed form, has not been published. See idem, *Die deuteronomistische Redaktion des Buches Jeremia* (Die Humboldt-Universität, Berlin, 1970).
4. Major omissions from this redaction are the oracles against the foreign nations (chaps. 46—51), chap. 52, drawn from 2 Kings 25, and a few other later redactional additions (= PD).

tor(s) edited previously transmitted words and "self-reports" of Jeremiah (the so-called A materials), as well as reports about the prophet (the so-called B materials).[5] The D contribution to these A and B materials consists in the addition of phrases, or even of an occasional sermon (e.g. 7:1—8:3), and in the arrangement of the whole. The prose sermons themselves are not from a source C,[6] but they are interpretive speeches composed in the process of redaction. By eliminating the redactional elements from the materials labeled A, B, and C by the source critics, we can often discover a tradition that differs from the Deuteronomistic redaction in language, form, and content. These materials are the closest we can come to the "real" Jeremiah, and they will form the basis for our discussion of the prophet's own reaction to exile.[7]

JEREMIAH'S RESPONSE TO EXILE:
CERTAINTY OF PERSONAL DELIVERANCE

Jeremiah was a vicarious fellow sufferer with Israel in its final days. His whole body shook at the thought of the enemy's attack

5. Gunther Wanke, *Untersuchungen zur sogenannten Baruchschrift*, BZAW 122 (Berlin: Walter de Gruyter, 1971), argues that the B materials consist of three separate cycles: (*a*) 37—44; (*b*) 19:1—20:6; 26; 27; 28; 29; 36; and (*c*) 45 and 51:59–64.

6. Helga Weippert, *Die Prosareden des Jeremiabuches*, BZAW 132 (Berlin: Walter de Gruyter, 1973), denies that type C materials come from a Deuteronomistic redactor. She does not however adequately distinguish between Deuteronomic language (that of the book of Deuteronomy itself) and Deuteronomistic language (that is, the language of the theologians who were indebted to Deuteronomy but who also had experienced the transforming effects of the death of Josiah, the failure of his reform, the fall of Judah, the burning of the temple, etc.). For an English summary of Wanke and Weippert see William L. Holladay, "A Fresh Look at 'Source B' and 'Source C' in Jeremiah," *VT* 25 (1975): 394–412. Holladay basically accepts Weippert's conclusions.

7. There are two major difficulties with Thiel's work: (1) He consistently argues that the LXX omitted passages from its Hebrew *Vorlage*, whereas J. Gerald Janzen, *Studies in the Text of Jeremiah* (Cambridge, Mass.: Harvard University Press, 1973), has demonstrated that the shorter text of LXX is often superior, that is, more original, from a text-critical standpoint. (2) Thiel believes that the D redaction is unified, or at least that it took place at one time and in one locale. For a more differentiated view, see provisionally Karl-Ferdinand Pohlmann, *Studien zum Jeremiabuch*, FRLANT 118 (Göttingen: Vandenhoeck & Ruprecht, 1978).

(4:19–21), and he cried out when he saw the people's suffering (14:17–18). Thrown in the stocks (chap. 20), endangered after his temple address (chap. 26), harassed by rival prophets (chap. 28), imprisoned during the final siege (chaps. 37—38), and taken to Egypt after 587 against his will (chaps. 42—44), Jeremiah bore suffering for the word he proclaimed even as that word suffered at the hands of King Jehoiakim (chap. 36).

Nowhere is Jeremiah's suffering more clear than in his "confessions."[8] He suffered from persecutors whose attacks were really aimed at Yahweh (15:15). God's word was his joy and delight, but it also brought loneliness and a disquietude that reflected God's wrath against Israel (15:16–17). Worst of all, God seemed to him untrustworthy and deceitful (15:18).

God's answer to Jeremiah's complaints was a hard gospel. It offered no escape (cf. 12:5) but called on the prophet to repent (15:19) and promised him more of the same kind of ministry. He was to be unyielding and hard, strong enough to survive future attacks. Certainty would come only from simple words of assurance: "I am with you, to save you and deliver you . . . out of the hand of the wicked" (15:20b–21). This same "gospel" appears also in the account of Jeremiah's call (1:8). Through these assurances of his own salvation Jeremiah attained insights into the nature of God. Despite suffering severely under the demands of his office, Jeremiah knew that he himself would be saved and not abandoned.[9]

GOOD NEWS FOR THE NORTHERN EXILES

Jeremiah's first response to the experience of exile dealt with the exile of the northern kingdom, which had been captured by Assyria nearly a century before his ministry began. Many scholars link his hope oracles directed to the north with Josiah's attempt to reoccupy the northern territory. However that may be, we find in these passages the same call for repentance and the same limited deliverance that were directed to the prophet himself:

8. Jer. 11:18—12:6; 15:10–11, 15–21; 17:14–18; 18:18–23; 20:7–13 and 14–18. Note also Yahweh's anguish over the necessity of punishing his people (12:7).
9. Cf. 1:18–19 and Herrmann, *Heilserwartungen,* 231–32.

Return, faithless Israel, says Yahweh.
I will not look on you in anger,
    for I am merciful, says Yahweh;
I will not be angry for ever.
Only acknowledge your guilt.
                                        (3:12–13)[10]

Two passages from the book of consolation (30—31) are commonly interpreted as messages of hope to the north, dating from early in Jeremiah's ministry. The first (31:2–6) grounds north Israel's hope in the everlasting love and faithfulness of Yahweh (v. 3; cf. 3:12 and Exod. 33:12–17). In a distant country the erstwhile northerners will receive the promise of a return to the land (= rest in v. 2). Joy and celebration (v. 4b) will replace present suffering (cf. 13b); successful harvests (v. 5) will come instead of the constant agricultural frustration that had been Israel's lot (Amos 5:11). Once more a call for a pilgrimage to Zion will sound on the hills of Ephraim (v. 6), that is, right in the midst of the northern kingdom. This stress on the cultic unity of all Israel may reflect the influence of Josiah's reform. In any case, it would seem to antedate Jeremiah's harsh critique of the temple in 605 (cf. chaps. 7 and 26).

The second passage (31:15–22) reports north Israel's repentance (vv. 18–19) and Yahweh's subsequent love (v. 20). Ephraim is promised a return from the enemy's land to his own homeland (vv. 16–17). His contrition and sorrow come in response to Yahweh's punishment (v. 19); they are God's answer to his prayer for restoration (v. 18). Even when Yahweh speaks words of judgment over his son Ephraim, he can't help remembering him. Fond feelings for his son overflow at the mention of his name.

In these passages we find references to God's mercy, his time-limited anger, and his love and faithfulness. Israel's repentance is stressed in 3:12–13 and 31:15–20. Jeremiah's message to the

---

10. Thiel, *Jeremia 1—25*, pp. 83–91, holds that the present form of 3:6–18 is the product of D but considers the above words to be authentic Jeremianic material. Literary critical judgments in this chapter will follow Thiel unless otherwise indicated.

exiles of north Israel, therefore, was only an extension of that deliverance he experienced in his own embattled life.

JEREMIAH'S MESSAGE TO JUDAH: SUBMIT TO BABYLON

Sometime after the first deportation in 597, Jeremiah performed a symbolic act which indicated his understanding of Judah's immediate future. In 594/593 envoys from Edom, Moab, Ammon, Tyre, and Sidon had come to Jerusalem to plan a concerted revolt against Babylon. Jeremiah put on yoke-bars at Yahweh's direction and promised all who submitted to the yoke of the king of Babylon that they would be able to continue living in their land (27:2–4, 11).

The prophet's action led to an intense conflict with Hananiah, a fellow Benjaminite. Hananiah had good credentials—his name itself testified to his Yahwistic faith, he introduced his message with a "Thus says Yahweh," and he even performed a symbolic act by breaking the yoke-bars from Jeremiah's neck (vv. 10–14)—but his message directly contradicted Jeremiah's. According to Hananiah, Yahweh would break the yoke (dominion) of Nebuchadnezzar and within two years bring back not only the temple vessels but also king Jehoiachin and the others deported in 597.

Jeremiah conceded that Hananiah's words sounded good (28:6), but he noted that previous prophets had consistently prophesied war, famine, and pestilence. A prophet who promised a bright future would only be credible when his words became facts in history (cf. Deut. 18:21–22). When Hananiah broke the yoke-bars, Jeremiah silently went his way; he had no word of Yahweh for this occasion (cf. 42:7). When that word of Yahweh came, Jeremiah put on bars of iron to symbolize the inescapable servitude of all nations to the king of Babylon. He rebuked Hananiah, charging that this false prophet had not been sent by Yahweh and that he had made the people trust a lie. Hananiah's death at Yahweh's hand would come within the year. A mere two months later, according to the narrator, that sentence became reality.

This story of prophetic conflict illustrates the difficulty for

prophet and people in the early years of exile in knowing what
the will of Yahweh was, but this incident also indicates that there
were right and wrong options, after all, and the wrong ones could
come with all the good credentials of a Hananiah. However
despicable the prophets were who prophesied by Baal (23:13; 2:8)
or who participated in adultery (23:14; 29:23) or other ungodli-
ness (23:11, 15), it is hard to believe that *they* were a central
challenge to a prophet like Jeremiah or the faith of the people.
A false prophet like Hananiah, on the other hand, formed the
real challenge. Such false prophets were dangerous because they
strengthened the hands of the evildoers, thus keeping them from
repentance (23:14). A person who had really stood in God's council (cf. 23:18, 22) would turn people from their evil way (23:22).
The dreams of the false prophets made people forget God's
name (23:27). Worse yet, they offered vain hopes (23:16) or
"Peace, peace" where there was no peace (6:14=8:11). Hananiah
and his colleagues among the false prophets refused to face the
realities of history, and they reassured unrepentant Israel with
vapid promises. No wonder the people loved it (5:31)! For the
Judeans between 597 and 587, cheap forgiveness and an easy
escape from Nebuchadnezzar's army were no word from God—
so said Jeremiah. Those who had already begun their exile were
the good figs; the remnant left in Judah were like bad, unedible
figs (24:1a, 2–4, 5*, 8*) [11]

A call to submit to Babylon, to say yes to the reality and ap-
propriateness of God's judgment—that was Jeremiah's and God's
word as the shades of exile fell. It was the word offered to the
surrounding nations in the symbolic action of chaps. 27 and 28.
Though the prophet promised continued dwelling on its land to
any nation which would submit to the Babylonian king (27:11),
Jeremiah elsewhere urged simple surrender or desertion to the
enemy (21:9; cf. 38:2), a strategy apparently followed by not a
few (38:19; 39:9). He prophesied that the city of Jerusalem would
be given to the Babylonian army (38:3), a message which his
opponents saw as traitorous since it weakened the hands of the

11. These verses contain the pre-D tradition about the two baskets of figs
and its meaning. Per contra Thiel, *Jeremia 1—25*, p. 259.

soldiers (38:4). Better to weaken the soldiers' hands, the prophet might say, than to strengthen the hands of the evildoers in the fashion of the false prophets (23:14). Jeremiah saw no hope in the temporary lifting of the siege caused by an Egyptian relief force. No, he knew the Egyptians would retreat and the Chaldeans would burn the city. Even if—by some superhuman efforts —the Judeans would defeat the whole Chaldean army and reduce the attackers to casualties lying in their tents, these wounded would still get up and burn the city with fire (37:3-10).

But when Jerusalem fell and Jeremiah was hailed before the Babylonian authorities, he decided to stay in the land (40:4-6). Hence Jeremiah was no political opportunist, trimming his sails to the prevailing Babylonian winds. Instead, he saw Babylon's victory over Jerusalem as God's own act of judgment, richly deserved and to be welcomed by all, the sooner the better. Surrendering to Babylon was the only logical and theological consequence to be drawn from an analysis of Judah's idolatrous infidelity (chaps. 2—3) and her superstitious trust in the temple (chaps. 7 and 26). The "enemy from the north," whose advent Jeremiah had announced with fear and trembling in his earliest oracles, showed up at Yahweh's direction in 587 B.C. Hailing Jerusalem's fall, anticipating it, and even helping folks to desert was not a popular or easy prophetic task. But it was an essential, even crucial reaction to and interpretation of the onrushing exile.

BABYLON'S FUTURE IS YOUR FUTURE

In a remarkable letter to those who had been deported to Babylon in 597, Jeremiah rejected any hope for a return from exile (29:4-7). Instead, he urged the people to settle down for the long haul. They should build houses and live in them, plant gardens and eat their produce, take wives and have children, and marry off these sons and daughters. Jeremiah even advised the people to pray for Babylon—in its prosperity would be the prosperity of the exiles.

This advice to pray indicated that worship—without temple and cult—was possible for the Israelites in the unclean land of Babylon. Secondly, it gave strong endorsement to the Babylonian hegemony. Israel's material prosperity would be directly proportional to that of Babylon. Praying for Babylon was in Israel's self-interest. Thirdly, however, it urged prayer for Israel's *enemy*. Jeremiah's personal experiences may have helped shape this counsel. Faced with people who had dug a pit for his life he had interceded for them with God so that God's anger might turn away (18:20). Now he urged the exiles to pray also for public enemy number one.

Jeremiah's advice about houses, gardens, and marriage suggests that he considered it possible to survive in a land which other people would have called unclean (Amos 7:17; Hos. 9:1ff.). This survival, moreover, was a long-range proposition—a house or a family is not built in a few days! In a sense, Jeremiah said that exile should be home, that there would be no reversing the collapse begun in 597. The very best "figs" were those who had already begun the exile (24:4–5). This realistic but radical message had vigorous opponents among the exiles in Babylon, just as Hananiah opposed Jeremiah in Palestine. Two "prophets," Ahab and Zedekiah, were accused by Jeremiah of prophesying a lie that would lead to their execution by Nebuchadnezzar (29:21). While we are not told the content of their prophecy, the context in Jeremiah and Nebuchadnezzar's vicious reaction in roasting them with fire (v. 22) suggest that they proclaimed Babylon's imminent demise. Jeremiah's word was not the only "word of God" to which the exiles were treated!

Did Jeremiah himself say there would be *no* return from exile, or only that the exile would be quite prolonged? Two passages are crucial in this discussion. The first (29:10–14) promises a return to the land after seventy years are completed for Babylon, but the vocabulary here is strongly Deuteronomistic. Thiel has suggested that the number seventy might have occurred to the D redactor about 550 when the rise of Cyrus began to reveal Babylon's clay feet. The other uses of the number seventy in chap. 25 (vv. 11–12) are in verses probably added when the oracles against the foreign nations were incorporated into the Book of Jeremiah sometime *after* the main D redaction.[12] The limitation of Babylon's power to three generations (27:7) is congruent with a

12. Cf. Thiel, *Jeremia 1—25*, p. 273.

seventy-year rule for Babylon, but the verse containing this information is absent from the LXX and, therefore, probably not authentic. In short, 29:10–14, because of its Deuteronomistic language, as well as 25:11–12 and 27:7, because of their probable late date, cannot be used to show that Jeremiah himself prophesied a return from the Exile and an end to the Babylonian power.

The symbolic act recorded in the second key passage (51:59–64), however, does announce the eventual fall of Babylon and thus imply the deliverance of the exiles. The passage describes a delegation *sent* by (so LXX) or *accompanied* by (so MT) Zedekiah to Babylon in 594–593. Jeremiah sent along a book announcing evil against Babylon and asked Seraiah, the brother of Baruch (32:12), to read it aloud, then tie a stone to it, and throw it into the Euphrates. As this book would sink, so would Babylon also one day sink.[13]

To sum up: Jeremiah's letter urged the exiles to settle down for a long stay in Babylon. There would be no quick return home, no escaping the judgment brought by Nebuchadnezzar. House building, agriculture, family life, and prayer, on the other hand, should go on in Babylon with blessing. At the same time, if 51:59–64 is authentic, Jeremiah believed in the eventual downfall of Babylon, an idea expanded into a new gift of the land by the D redaction in 29:10–14 and other passages. Finally, and in any case, his letter indicates that exile was not prison. Normal life could go on, apparently with some freedom.

AND YET, THE LAND

During the final siege of Jerusalem Jeremiah performed an incredible act of faith, as we learn from one of his self-reports (32:6b–15). His cousin, Hanamel, came to him with a request to buy his field in Anathoth according to the law of redemption (Lev. 25:25). Hanamel must have been in danger of losing his property because of a bad debt. Jeremiah willingly played the

13. To retain this symbolic act for the pre-D Jeremiah one can propose that it was a private rather than a public message like his letter, dealing with the distant future rather than the present. There are redactional ties to its present context in vv. 60b, 62, and 64 (cf. 50:3 and 51:26b).

role of kinsman-redeemer, paid the appropriate price, and carried through elaborate procedures to certify the transaction. Then he entrusted the two copies of the deed to Baruch and commanded him to store them in a clay jar so that they could be preserved for a long time.

Thus, despite the impending judgment of 587 with its attendant reversal of the promise of the land, Jeremiah affirmed—on Yahweh's authority—that normal business transactions would one day resume (32:15). To make his actions as loud as his word he bought a field in that land "in advance." The prophet's ambivalent attitude toward the land would seem to echo his ambivalence toward Babylon noted in 29:5–7 and 51:59–64. His affirmation of an eventual future for the promised land may also help explain why he refused to go to Babylon (despite his counseling others to desert to the Chaldeans, 40:4–6), his bitter opposition to the proposed flight to Egypt after the assassination of Gedaliah (42:17), and his oracle, once he got there, announcing Nebuchadnezzar's forthcoming victory over Egypt, in which he would hand over to captivity those doomed to it (43:8–13).

THE FUTURE OF KINGSHIP

Outside of Josiah, whom the prophet praised for his justice (22:15–16), Jeremiah has little good to say about the kings who ruled in his day. He urged only mourning for Jehoahaz, who was deported to Egypt in 609, and he asserted that this king would never return alive (22:10–12). Jehoiakim is virtually his whipping boy, criticized for his mindless palace renovations during days of national crisis and his social injustice (22:13–19; cf. 21:11–14), not to mention his burning of the scroll of Jeremiah's words (chap. 36). Jeremiah announced that Jehoiakim's body would be cast forth unburied and he would have no successors (26:19; 36:30). Jehoiachin, too, comes under judgment: he and his sons will never reign again in Judah (22:28–30). The best that can be said for weak Zedekiah is that his certain defeat and exile will be followed by a peaceful death (34:3–5).

In view of this exceedingly negative experience with kingship, why would Jeremiah give the monarchy any role in the future?

The surprising number of passages dealing with this theme in the present Book of Jeremiah can be quite deceptive. At best only one or two of them can be attributed to Jeremiah himself.

We read on two occasions, for example, of future kings who will sit on the throne of David, riding chariots and horses (17:25; 22:4), but both passages are in Deuteronomistic contexts and make the existence of these future kings dependent on the people's obedience. Neither passage can be attributed to Jeremiah. A prose insert in 30:8–9 speaks of people serving Yahweh their God and David their king, but this passage too is assigned to Deuteronomistic (Nicholson) or post-Deuteronomistic (Thiel) hands. No strong objections can be brought against the authenticity of 30:18–21. Since these poetic verses speak quite generally about the future, however, it is difficult to assign them to a specific period in Jeremiah's ministry. The promised future prince or ruler (v. 21), to be sure, will be a native Israelite (cf. Deut. 17:15), but the relationship, if any, of the coming monarch to the Davidic line or to kingship in the strict sense of the word is completely unmentioned. His duties seem to be primarily liturgical.

The central passage—and central problem—in any discussion of a future king in Jeremiah is 23:5–6. These verses are part of a larger redactional unit (21:1—23:8) dealing with kingship. After a collection of negative words about specific kings, the first four verses of chap. 23 utter woe to the bad shepherds or rulers and promise that Yahweh will set up new shepherds who will really care for the flock (cf. 3:15). Vv. 7–8 round off the unit by referring to a future exodus from the north country. Both vv. 1–4 and 7–8 are filled with Deuteronomistic language and can be assigned to the hand of D.[14] Though vv. 5–6 do not show such Deuteronomistic language, their specific messianic promises form a sequel to the general promise of new shepherds in vv. 1–4; there is also a key word (*Stichwort*) connection between *wahăqī-mōtî* in v. 4 and the identical word in v. 5. In short, the pres-

14. Thiel, *Jeremia 1—25*, pp. 246–49. He believes that vv. 5–6 were added after the D redaction.

ent redactional position presupposes the materials of D. The question is, Were vv. 5–6 composed by the D redactor (or even later), or are they part of the pre-D tradition?[15]

The principal positive argument for authenticity is the possible play on words in v. 6: The king's new name, *yhwh ṣidqēnû*, can be seen as a pun on the name Zedekiah, *ṣidqîyāhû*. The messiah's name would be "Zedekiah-written-backwards": he would be the direct opposite of this puppet king, practicing righteousness where he did not. The remaining parts of vv. 5–6 seem most appropriate in the time of Jeremiah:

a. "He shall reign as king and deal wisely." This clause contrasts the messiah's true kingship with the puppet kingship of Zedekiah. An alternate translation of "righteous branch" (v. 5) is "legitimate branch," an implicit criticism of Zedekiah's credentials.

b. "He shall execute justice and righteousness in the land." This promise would have the injustice of Jehoiakim as its foil (22:13–17).

c. "Judah and Israel will be safe in his days." This contrasts with the siege and defeat of Jerusalem in the time of Zedekiah.

d. Yahweh's assignment of the messiah's name can be understood as a none-too-subtle critique of Zedekiah, who had been known as Mattaniah until the king of Babylon renamed him (2 Kings 24:17). The new king would get his name from God himself.

An important argument for a date prior to the D redaction is the silence of this passage about the relationship of the messiah to the Deuteronomic law. The Book of Deuteronomy itself ordered the king to copy the law and read it daily (17:18–20). Finally, this passage must be dated early enough so that the term "branch" (*ṣemaḥ*) could be used by Zechariah as a messianic title around 520 B.C. (3:8 and 6:12).

---

15. Arguments against authenticity center on the negative attitude of Jeremiah toward the contemporary kings of Judah (e.g. Jehoiakim, 36:30; Jehoiachin, 22:30; and Zedekiah, 34:3–5). But in view of his announcement that the land would be lost to Babylon *and* that it would be possessed again (32:15), a paradoxical or ambivalent attitude toward kingship in Jeremiah should not occasion great surprise.

In arguing for the Jeremianic origin of this passage we have already touched on parts of its meaning. We should note in addition the theocentricity of the promise: it is Yahweh who will raise up the branch. Israel's security will come only "in the days of" this branch, not by virtue of his actions. The messianic name confirms this interpretation. It might be rendered, "It is Yahweh who will be the source of our vindication." The description of his rule mentions his wisdom and his justice, but not his military power.

In the future, Jeremiah seems to say, both north and south will be restored to safety and security. Then a king will rule, through God's grace, who will be a real king, practicing the kind of justice in society that legitimate kings should. His name points to the real ground of hope for that future. This interpretation of 23:5–6 harmonizes well with other words we have discussed from Jeremiah. The prophet's hope for personal deliverance and for deliverance of the north, his words about the end of Babylon and hope for the land—all of this presupposes a God whose anger does not last forever, who promises even as he announces judgment. When Yahweh is the judge, only Yahweh can be the source of vindication.[16]

THE REACTION TO EXILE IN JEREMIAH D

The Deuteronomistic redaction of Jeremiah (D) adapts the message of the prophet Jeremiah to the situation of exile on the basis of a theology informed by Deuteronomy and the Deuteronomistic History. D incorporated many authentic words of Jeremiah, including those we have discussed above. We would not want to deny the possibility that even in those sections which are almost entirely in Deuteronomistic language (type C), a word or idea of the prophet himself may have served a catalytic function, even if in most cases that Jeremianic kernel cannot be demonstrated with any certainty. We are primarily interested in how the D redaction gave a new reaction to the Exile through the mouth of Jeremiah.

16. See Ulrich Kellermann, *Messias und Gesetz*, BibSt 61 (Neukirchen-Vluyn: Neukirchener Verlag, 1971), and M. Weinfeld, "Jeremiah and the Spiritual Metamorphoses of Israel," *ZAW* 88 (1976) : 17–56. Jer. 23:5–6 is interpreted at length in 33:14–26, but this passage is absent from the LXX and secondary.

587 IS YAHWEH'S RESPONSE TO
THE PEOPLE'S SIN

One function of the D redaction is to defend Yahweh against the charge of neglect, powerlessness, or unfairness. D begins this theodicy by leaving no doubt about who was the *real destroyer* of Jerusalem. Consider Yahweh's threat to Zedekiah during the final siege. "I myself will fight against you with outstretched hand and strong arm, in anger, and in fury, and in great wrath" (21:5). D lets the captain of the guard be his spokesman in 40:3: "Yahweh has brought it about [the destruction of Jerusalem] and has done as he said."

Yahweh is the agent, but Israel's sin is the cause for the disaster of 587. Given the circumstances, according to D, Yahweh had little choice: "Yahweh could no longer bear your evil doings and the abominations which you committed" (44:22; cf. 11:8b). Exilic Israel could not claim lack of warning, for D repeatedly records the warnings given Israel by the prophets throughout her history, warnings which always went unheeded.[17] Even the most recent prophet, Jeremiah, whom D compared to Moses, offered the Judeans a chance to repent and thus experience God's forgiveness (36:3; cf. 7:27; 18:11–12; 26:3–4, 13; 36:7, 31), but the people refused also to listen to him.

D continued his indictment of the people by surrounding the reports of the sufferings of Jeremiah and of the word of God during and following Jerusalem's fall (chaps. 37—44) with accounts of Jehoiakim's perfidy in burning the scroll of the prophet (chap. 36) *and* of Baruch's fidelity (chap. 45), both of which occurred in 605. Jehoiakim and the people brought on Jerusalem's catastrophe by their attitude toward the message of the prophets (36:3, 31); faithful Baruch, on the other hand, gained his life as a prize of war. Similarly, Ebed-Melech, Jeremiah's Ethiopian accomplice, was granted life because of his trust in Yahweh (39:18), evidenced by his actions toward Jeremiah (38:7–13), but the king and people fell to the Babylonian armies. D's message is clear: listening to the prophet could have led to life for all just as it did in fact save the lives of Baruch and Ebed-Melech.

Meanwhile, the people were anything but deaf to the words of the false prophets. Though neither sent nor commanded by Yahweh, these preachers of lies told the people there would be no sword or famine. "Peace is sure," they cried, and the people believed them. These false prophets and the people who listened to them deserved and got a brutal death in Jerusalem, with none to bury them.[18] Since they spoke words which did not happen, since they utilized divination and dreams, they really deserved the fate they received. We know that such "salvation" or false prophets continued their activity in the early part of the Exile (cf. 28:21–23). D views them as insidious opponents of Jeremiah whose success with priests and people was a primary cause of exile.

At the center of D's theological critique, however, is the people's stubborn and persistent breaking of the covenant made at the time of the Exodus (Jer. 11:6–8). That covenant, according to the Deuteronomistic History, consisted of the Decalogue and its authoritative interpretation in the Book of Deuteronomy. The D redaction of Jeremiah has a similar view of the covenant as can be seen by its additions to chap. 34. The pre-D tradition had reported an incident during the final siege of Jerusalem in which the king and the people had made a "covenant" to emancipate all their slaves, perhaps in an attempt to enlist their support in the final struggle. Later the people reneged on this covenant and were put under a curse (34:8b, 9a*, 10–13a, 18*).[19] D reinterpreted this "ad hoc covenant" by making additions in vv. 8a, 9b, and 13b–17. The covenant now became an agreement to carry out the specific injunctions of Deuteronomy (especially 15:1, 12). The people's perfidy was a violation of *the* covenant, meriting nothing short of sword, pestilence, and famine. Such perfidy only continued that done by the fathers right from the start (34:14;

---

18. Cf. 27:9–10, 14–18. "False prophets" became a kind of code word for opponents of Jeremiah, leading D to include Pashhur and Shemaiah also among their number. Cf. Thiel, *Jeremia 1—25*, pp. 227–29, and idem, *Die Redaktion des Buches*, pp. 472–74.

19. Thiel, *Die Redaktion des Buches*, pp. 527–38.

cf. 11:8). D's description of idolatry as "following after other gods" (11:10; cf. 13:10, 35:15, and often) shows his clear focus on the Decalogue and Deuteronomy as the relevant measuring sticks. The year 587 was the just and expectable result of violating the covenant made with the fathers.

Despite Israel's violation of the covenant, D indicates that the events of 587 could still have been avoided. In editing the temple address and its aftermath, he made two crucial additions to the words of Yahweh (26:3) and Jeremiah (26:13), which indicated that Yahweh would change his mind about destroying Jerusalem if the people would turn from their evil ways. But the necessary repentance never came. Even after 587, according to D, God offered a way to escape: "If you will remain in this land, then I will build you up . . . for I repent of the evil which I did to you" (42:10). The promise of a new beginning for those who would remain in the land was rejected by that group that took Jeremiah to Egypt against his will. Hence the destruction of their refuge in Egypt too seemed fully justified in D's theology (24:8; 42:10–17; 44:11–14).[20] The remnant in Jerusalem had been like the "nation" in 18:9–10, concerning which God had declared that he would build and plant it but which had not listened to his voice, leading God to repent of the good which he had intended to do. Israel's failure to take advantage of God's offer of mercy before and after 587 made fully clear the theological reason why God gave Nebuchadnezzar victory in Jerusalem in 587 and why God gave him victory over Egypt, the refuge for some Jewish deportees, in 569–568.

D also justified the judgment in a series of passages displaying a catechetical or a question-answer style. The question in each case is, Why has the judgment happened? The answer: Because they have abandoned Yahweh (5:19; 16:11), his Torah (9:12; 16:11), or his covenant (22:9); because they have not listened to him (9:12; 16:12); or because they have fallen away to other gods

---

20. The polemic against the flight to Egypt goes back to Jeremiah himself (42:17; 43:8–12), but D used this material differently from the inherited tradition; that is, he used it to justify God's *past* acts of destruction. Jeremiah himself warned of *coming* destruction for the refugees in Egypt.

(5:19; 9:13; 16:11)—all stated in the vocabulary of the Deuteronomists. In 9:13 and 16:12 the sin of the present generation is compared to that of the fathers.[21] These pericopes served D's purpose of theodicy well. Yahweh had not lost his power or forgotten his righteousness. Rather, Israel's guilt was the cause of their present miseries, and their guilt extended from the period of the fathers at the time of the Exodus until the present day.

The evil of the present generation, more abundant even than that of the fathers (16:12; cf. 7:26), is one of D's replies to an apparently common exilic complaint against collective retribution:

> The fathers have eaten sour grapes,
> and the children's teeth are set on edge.
> (31:29; cf. Ezek. 18:2)

D's allegation that the last generation is worse than the first made short shrift of this complaint about exile. At the same time D promised that this proverb would not be used in the future because everyone would then be punished only for his own sins (31:29–30).[22] In 32:18–19 D sets side by side an assertion of the old doctrine of retribution *and* its correction: "[You, Yahweh, are the one who] dost requite the guilt of the fathers to their children after them" (v. 18), and "rewarding everyone according to his own ways" (v. 19). In several ways, then, D took cognizance of the problems of collective retribution but maintained that such theological niceties are irrelevant to the complaints of his present audience: their sins, worse than their fathers', fully justified the events of 587, of which Yahweh was the unabashed author.

HOPE FOR THOSE IN THE LAND

The prophet Jeremiah himself had hoped for some kind of future existence in the land. We learn this from his purchase of the field of Hanamel (32:15), from his polemic against the flight

---

21. See Thiel, *Jeremia 1—25*, pp. 295–300, where he deals with 5:19; 9:11–15; 16:10–13. Cf. 22:8–9, Deut. 29:23–27, and 1 Kings 9:8–9.
22. See Weinfeld, "Jeremiah," *ZAW* 88 (1976) : 35–39.

to Egypt (42:17, 43:8–12), and from his refusal to accept the offer of amnesty in Babylon (40:4–6). D developed this notion in a literary form which seems to reflect another specific preaching style practiced in the Exile.[23]

1. 22:1–5. The choice set before the exiles in this passage deals with what we would call social justice: deliverance from oppressors, kindness to resident aliens, orphans, and widows; and abstaining from bloodshed. Those who would obey this word were assured of a salvation appropriate for exiles: Davidic kings, with their chariots and horses, their servants, and their people, would enter the gates of the royal palace once more. In short, the normal life of preexilic Israel would be restored. Failure to practice justice would lead to punishment.[24] D's redaction of Jeremiah's temple address (7:1–15) had a very similar concern with social justice (7:5–6), and it promised, too, continued normal existence in the land (7:7).

2. 17:19–27.[25] D again puts the emphasis on obedient listening, this time obedience to the Sabbath regulations. If the Sabbath were kept, kings, their officials, and the general population would regularly use the city gates (17:25), and Jerusalem would be inhabited forever. In fact, people would come from all over Judah and Benjamin to bring a full array of sacrificial offerings to the temple. Disobedience would end again in destruction (cf. v. 27).

In offering a future based on obedience, D put forth a message he ascribed to all eras of Israel's history. God had always said, "Turn now, every one of you, from his evil way and wrong doings, and dwell upon the land which Yahweh has given to you and your fathers from of old and for ever" (25:5; cf. 35:15).

---

23. Three clear examples of this "alternative sermon" appear in the present text of D: 7:1–15; 17:19–27; 22:1–5. For discussion of this form and its structure see Thiel, *Jeremia 1—25*, pp. 290–95.

24. Instead of including the actual judgments appropriate to an exilic sermon, D used threats that looked forward to 587. He thereby turned the reader's attention to the situation of the historical Jeremiah.

25. The historical Jeremiah would hardly have promised a happy future on the basis of obedience to cultic demands like Sabbath keeping. Thiel, *Jeremia 1—25*, pp. 202–9, and Nicholson, *Preaching to the Exiles*, 124–25, support an exilic, rather than the frequently proposed postexilic, date.

SALVATION FOR THE EXILES

D begins his supplement to Jeremiah's letter to the exiles with these startling words: "When seventy years are completed for Babylon, I will visit you, and I will fulfill to you my promise and bring you back to this place" (29:10). Thus instead of following Jeremiah and rejecting any hope for a return from exile, D announced that exile would have a happy ending. Defeat for Babylon (cf. 27:7), a new exodus and gift of the land, and a fuller picture of the new monarchy that would replace the previous corrupt one—these form the motifs of D's advance over Jeremiah. Such an advance is, in D's view, God's keeping of his word. The principal passages involved are 23:1–8; 24:6–7; 29:10–14; and 32:37–41.

Perhaps the best place to begin is 23:1–8, D's summation of and reaction to the oracles against the kings of Judah (21:11—22:30). These kings, D says, had scattered ($p\hat{u}\d{s}$, Hiphil) Yahweh's flock; they had driven his sheep away ($n\bar{a}dah$, Hiphil) and had not given them proper supervision ($p\bar{a}qad$, Qal). Remarkably, D goes on to confess that Yahweh is really the one that drove away his people ($n\bar{a}dah$, vv. 3 and 8);[26] he is the one who executed judgmental supervision ($p\bar{a}qad$, Qal) over the shepherds (v. 2); aye, he is the one who—according to a D passage in another context (9:16)—scattered the people ($p\hat{u}\d{s}$, Hiphil). By using the identical verbs for the effects of Yahweh's judgmental actions and the kings' sinful ones, D suggested that Yahweh was indeed the *agent* of destruction, but the kings' sins were the ultimate *cause*.

The intricate and balanced use of verbs continues in the *promises* of these verses. Yahweh, who had dealt out punishments appropriate to the kings' crimes, would gather those he himself had scattered and would raise up new shepherds who would do what kings should do—shepherd their sheep (v. 4). Yahweh's visiting of the iniquity of the evil shepherds (23:2) would be balanced by his saving visiting of the exiles (29:10). His driving

---

26. Cf. 8:3; 16:15; 24:9, 10; 27:10, 15; 29:14, 18; and 32:37, where the driving away of Israel is always attributed to Yahweh.

away of his people would be matched by his bringing them back from the place where he had driven them (23:3 and 8). To stress the fact that Yahweh's salvific will is as strong as his judgmental actions, D uses similar metaphors or identical verbs to express *both* aspects of God's behavior. The best expression of this theology is in 31:28, also to be assigned to D: "And it shall come to pass that *as I have watched over them* to pluck up and break down, to overthrow, to destroy, and bring evil, *so I will watch over them* to build and to plant."[27]

The first Exodus was highly important for D (cf. e.g. 7:22; 11:4; 31:32; 32:21), but this redactor asserted that in the future, references to the Exodus in oath formulas would be radically transformed. No longer would people say, "As Yahweh lives who brought up the house of Israel from the land of Egypt," but instead they would swear, "As Yahweh lives who brought in the descendants of Israel out of the north country and out of all the countries where he had driven them" (vv. 7–8; RWK, following LXX). The new exodus would be followed by a return to the land (cf. 24:6; 27:22; 29:10; 30:3), where the people would dwell securely (23:8; 30:3; 32:37). In the words of 32:41, "I will plant them in the land faithfully," that is, without the danger of further exile (cf. Amos 9:15). This renewed possession of the land would fulfill the promise first made to the fathers (30:3; cf. 16:15). There (in the land) the people would be fruitful and multiply (cf. P).

D's promises to the exiles went well beyond those of the historical Jeremiah, yet they are considered to be the "keeping" of that earlier word of God. They also go beyond the Deuteronomistic History, where hopes for the future are spelled out with laconic reticence. Dtr had caused Solomon to pray, "Hear thou in heaven, and forgive the sin of thy people Israel, and bring them again to the land" (1 Kings 8:34). What Dtr expressed as hope clothed in prayer became explicit promise in the D redaction of Jeremiah. Yahweh promised both that people would pray and

27. Cf. 32:42. In Deut. 28:63 and Josh. 23:15 the construction is used in a negative sense, that is, God's bad word is as certain as his good.

that their prayers would be effective: "Then you will call upon me and come and pray to me, and I will hear you" (29:12).

Twice in the passages under discussion (that is, in 24:7 and 32:38) D mentions the so-called covenant formula ("They shall be my people and I will be their God"), and in 32:40 he refers to an everlasting covenant. Consequently, discussion of the famous new covenant passage in Jeremiah can be delayed no longer.

A NEW, EVERLASTING COVENANT[28]

The covenant promised in D was to be made in connection with the new exodus and gift of the land (32:36–41), but as a covenant with the house of Israel (31:31) it also included those who never experienced a geographical exile. The first covenant had been breached throughout Israel's history (31:32; cf. 11:10). This breach came despite the fact that Yahweh had been Israel's husband (31:32) or, as a literal translation might suggest, her "Baal"—he had given her everything she might expect from a fertility god, yet she had rejected him. D's new covenant would be different in that Yahweh would put his law in the people's midst and write it on their heart. It would not be inscribed on stones as something external. Rather, it would be the gift of one heart and one "way" to fear Yahweh for all days (32:39; cf. Ezek. 11:19; 18:31; 36:26). The new covenant in D differed from the old, not in that it was a covenant of "grace alone," without any expectation of obedience, but in that obedience would always be part of the covenant and in that the covenant would never be broken. Yahweh promised to implant his fear in Israel's hearts so that they would never turn away (32:40).

Such fear (chap. 32) or knowledge (chap. 31) of Yahweh is not learnable; it is a gift shared by all, rich and poor, young and old. To know Yahweh in the context of the Jeremiah book means to acknowledge him as Lord and to obey him. We can detect the specific connotation from Jeremiah's own comparison of Jehoiakim with his pious father Josiah:

---

28. For a demonstration of this covenant's Deuteronomistic provenance, see Thiel, *Die Redaktion des Buches*, pp. 496–506, and especially Herrmann, *Heilserwartungen,* pp. 179–85 and 195–204.

> He [Josiah] judged the cause of the poor and needy;
> then it was well.
> Is not this to *know* me?
>
> (22:16)

How is such a new covenant possible? D had gone out of the way to justify the judgmental actions of 587. They were the necessary consequences of Israel's sin, a sin raised to avalanche proportions by the present generation. How could a new, everlasting covenant be possible without contradicting the theodicy that had been one of D's major concerns?

The answer comes in the gracious intervention of God: "I will forgive their iniquity and remember their sin no more" (31:34).[29] In God's forgiveness, his wrath is counteracted; in God's forgetfulness is Israel's hope. Yet one does not experience in D the internal struggle between God's love and his wrath as in Hosea (11:8–9). Rather, "I will rejoice to do good to them" (32:41). Interestingly enough, each verse of the covenant pericope in 31:31–34 has a reference to the divine origin of the promise. Four times we are told this is an "oracle of Yahweh."

It may be well to itemize the ways in which the new covenant passages in Jeremiah D mark an advance within the Deuteronomistic movement and over against the prophet Jeremiah. (a) Deuteronomy had urged repentance while there was still time. Once the judgment of 587 fell, neither God's promise never to break the covenant (Judg. 2:1) nor a call for the people to return to the covenant was adequate. Only a new covenant, as in Jeremiah D, could resolve this dilemma. (b) Deuteronomy *demanded* that the law should be on the people's heart (6:6), but Jeremiah D presented obedience to the law as God's *gift,* either as the gift of a new heart or way (24:7; 32:39) or as God's writing the law upon the heart (31:33). (c) The words of the covenant in Deuteronomy were written on stones (4:13; 5:22; 10:2, 4); in Jeremiah D they are to be written on the heart. (d) While Deuteronomy uses terms like *Torah, statutes and judgments,* or *words* to describe the content of the covenant, the Deuteronomistic redactor

---

29. Elsewhere, D can connect forgiveness with prior repentance (36:3) or predicate the covenant relationship on Israel's turning around (24:7). Cf. also 1 Kings 8:37–39.

uses a Jeremiah word, *knowledge,* for this content. Yet Jeremiah
D differs from Jeremiah, who discussed the knowledge of God
only in laments about its absence or in accusations against Israel
(2:8; 4:22; 5:23; 9:2; 22:16). The knowledge of God for the redactor is regularly referred to as God's *future* gift (24:7; cf. 31:34).
(*e*) Deuteronomy stressed that the law must be taught and learned
(5:10, 14, etc.); in Jeremiah D such instruction is unnecessary.
The knowledge of Yahweh, in fact, will be present in all sectors
of society. (*f*) God's planting of Israel in the land in connection
with the new covenant takes place because he acts faithfully,
with all his heart and soul (32:41). To do something faithfully,
with all one's heart and soul, is attested in other Deuteronomistic
passages (1 Sam. 12:24; 1 Kings 2:4), but it is always used elsewhere of human activity. The Deuteronomistic redactor of Jeremiah moves beyond customary usage by ascribing such action to
Yahweh himself.

To sum up: The meaning of D's new covenant can be expressed in part by the "covenant formula": "They shall be my
people and I will be their God" (cf. 31:33; 32:38). But the new
covenant also inaugurates a new depth of fidelity to God's law:
an obedient heart is God's gift (32:39). The new covenant is not
breakable like the one made with the fathers; it is everlasting
both in God's commitment to it and in the people's response.
But it is a truly new covenant, subsequent to the broken first
one and exempt from its curses. God's forgiveness is the necessary
prerequisite for its initiation.

D AND THE NATIONS

The D redaction of the Book of Jeremiah did not yet contain
the oracles against the foreign nations in chaps. 46—51. However
early or late these oracles may be in whole or in part, they probably have nothing to tell us about the theology of D. Yet D's
failure to include such oracles should not hide the significance
of two positive words on the nations he does include.

1. 12:14–17. According to this passage, Israel's neighbors who
had encroached on her territory during her last days would be
exiled for this evil deed just as Judah had been exiled. Later,

Yahweh would have mercy and bring each nation—both Judah and the neighboring nations—back to its own land. If these nations would learn to swear "by Yahweh" (cf. 23:7-8), as they had taught preexilic Israel to swear "by Baal," they would be "built up" in the midst of "my people." The relationship of Israel to the nations is here resolved in such a way that the nations who confess Yahweh will share in the prosperous conditions enjoyed by the restored Israel.

2. 18:7-10. This passage, like the one above, deals with alternatives that are available for the nations. If God would announce his intention to pluck up, break down, and destroy a nation, and that nation would turn from its evil, Yahweh would change his mind about destruction (vv. 7-8). But Yahweh would also change his mind about the good which he had announced for a nation (his building and planting it) if it failed to listen to his voice (vv. 9-10). This second passage expands the horizon to include *any* nation (cf. 1:10), not just Israel's neighbors, and it makes clear that after the destruction of 587, Israel in principle holds no special advantage over the nations. Any nation can share in the good announced by Yahweh. Although neither of these passages goes as far as Second Isaiah or shares in the (later) hope for the pilgrimage of the nations to Zion, they are nevertheless remarkable expressions of openness toward the nations, including the neighbors who shared in pillaging Israel.

CONCLUSION

In this chapter we have surveyed the reactions to the Exile by the prophet Jeremiah and by that person or persons who edited his words (D) some thirty years or more after the prophet's final trip to Egypt. Jeremiah's own hopes were rather limited, though it is difficult to imagine how they could have been more dramatic. When he urged submission to Babylon, told the exiles to settle in for the long haul, promised a real king in the future instead of the puppetlike Zedekiah, or bought a field as an earnest for the day when business would resume—when he did these things he was controversial, daring, and full of faith. The editors of D had a somewhat different assignment in their day: to justify

God's governance of Israel, in part, but also to lay out new options both for those in the land and especially for those in exile. Others would carry farther D's hopes of a new exodus and a new possession of the land, and its new openness toward the nations. But it is difficult to imagine any passage within the Hebrew canon that did more to sketch the future with greater theological sophistication than D's announcement of a new covenant.

The transmitted words and reports of Jeremiah and the redactional work of D together form crucial voices from Israel's exile. Jeremiah urged acceptance of Babylon's rule and urged Israel to settle down in exile. D pointed out the justice of 587. Both then said yes to exile. But both also said no. Jeremiah's was a limited no, predicated on God's passing anger and clinging to the hope that there would yet be land to sell and a real king. D's was a fuller no to the Exile, with promises of a new exodus, a new taking of the land, a new covenant, and even new hope for the nations. Yes to exile—and no! So begins our survey of the prophetic response to the Exile.

CHAPTER 4

Yahweh Faithful and Free

Ezekiel's Response to Exile[1]

Among those deported from Jerusalem to Babylon in 597 were King Jehoiachin and Ezekiel the priest, the son of Buzi (1:3). Although Jehoiachin had ruled for only three months, his importance and power continued well into the Exile. Archaeologists have discovered seal impressions in Palestine inscribed with the words "Belonging to Eliakim, the steward of Yaukin," perhaps implying that Jehoiachin was recognized at least by some people as the legal king of Judah until the final destruction of 587.[2] In Babylonian documents Jehoiachin is mentioned as "the king of Judah," and it is reported that his five sons were given food from the royal storehouse. Thus, Jehoiachin retained his status as king even in exile. With the accession of Amel-Marduk to the Babylonian throne in 561, Jehoiachin was released from

1. See Walther Zimmerli, *Ezechiel*, BKAT 13 (Neukirchen-Vluyn: Neukirchener Verlag, 1955–69), and idem, the essays reprinted in *Gottes Offenbarung*, TBü 19 (München: Christian Kaiser, 1963), and *Studien zur alttestamentlichen Theologie und Prophetie*, TBü 51 (München: Christian Kaiser, 1974). Also useful are the commentaries of Walther Eichrodt, *Ezekiel*, OTL (Philadelphia: Westminster Press, 1970), and John W. Wevers, *Ezekiel*, NCB (Greenwood, S.C.: Attic Press, 1969). Among comparative studies we refer to Dieter Baltzer, *Ezechiel und Deuterojesaja*, BZAW 121 (Berlin and New York: Walter de Gruyter, 1971), and Thomas M. Raitt, *A Theology of Exile: Judgment/Deliverance in Jeremiah and Ezekiel* (Philadelphia: Fortress Press, 1977).

2. See the discussion by Bustenay Oded, *Israelite and Judaean History*, ed. J. H. Hayes and J. M. Miller, OTL (Philadelphia: Westminster Press, 1977), pp. 481–82. According to this theory, Eliakim administered the crown property of Jehoiachin.

69

prison and given special honors (2 Kings 25:27–30). If Jehoiachin
was considered the legitimate king even after his deportation,
it follows that Jehoiachin's uncle Zedekiah had no legitimate claims to the throne he occupied from 597 to 587, or
that, at the least, no hopes of deliverance from Babylon were to
be placed in him.

Ezekiel himself seems to have been of this opinion. Not only
do we find sharp words of criticism against Zedekiah and his
policies (17:5–6, 11–21; 21:25–26), but the dates scattered throughout the book reckon time from the exile of Jehoiachin (1:2; cf.
33:21; 40:1) and thus implicitly offer a snub to Zedekiah.

One can learn a great deal about the significance of Ezekiel
by studying the thirteen dates that are original in his book.[3]

a. Ezekiel's call occurred in 593. Although Zedekiah had loy-
ally gone on a mission to Babylon in 594 (Jer. 51:59), by mid-
summer 593 he had convened a group of rebel states in Jerusalem
(Jer. 27—28) whose optimistic hopes Jeremiah forcefully de-
nounced. If we can judge by the uncompromising announcement
of judgment against Judah and Jerusalem in chapters 1—24,
Ezekiel opposed this revolt with equal vigor. These two prophets
saw the historical inevitability of Nebuchadnezzar's victory and
theologically affirmed it.

b. The final date given in Ezekiel is 571 (29:17). While some
materials in the present book come from a later time, the prophet's ministry itself can be assigned roughly to 593–571. Ezekiel,
therefore, prophesied both before and after the final destruction
of Jerusalem in 587. He was a later contemporary of his Palestinian colleague Jeremiah (626–580s) and preceded Second Isaiah
(550–540) by nearly a generation. The latter fact accounts in part
for the far different emphasis and tone in the two prophets who
worked in the Babylonian Exile.

The oracle dated to 571 also helps us to see that Ezekiel was
able to change or modify an earlier word of God so that it would

3. See K. S. Freedy and D. B. Redford, "The Dates in Ezekiel in Relationship
to Biblical, Babylonian and Egyptian Sources," *JAOS* 90 (1970): 462–85. The
date in 24:1 MT is not original but was added from 2 Kings 25:1.

correspond to the actualities of history. According to 26:7ff., Tyre was to fall into the hands of Nebuchadnezzar and be totally destroyed. Despite a thirteen-year siege, however, the Babylonian king came up shorthanded: Tyre was not destroyed and plundered. To compensate Nebuchadnezzar for his trouble, Yahweh promised him the land of Egypt as his recompense (29:19–20). Thus Yahweh, according to Ezekiel's interpretation, remained faithful to his original promise, though he was free to adjust his word to fit the contingencies of history.

c. Three of the four visions in Ezekiel are given special emphasis by being supplied with dates (1:2; 8:1; 40:1).[4] Zimmerli sees symbolic significance in the year number (twenty-five) of the final vision (see below, n. 25).

d. Seven of the dates fall in the hectic tenth-twelfth years, that is, during the final siege of Jerusalem. Not incidentally, five of these are linked to oracles against Egypt. Egypt's meddling in Palestinian affairs was—as usual for those times—militarily fruitless and spiritually a disaster.

e. The oracle reporting the fall of Jerusalem is emphasized by providing it with a special date (33:21). This event marked a transition in Ezekiel's ministry from words of judgment against Judah and Jerusalem (chaps. 1—24) and against the nations (chaps. 25—32) to words of hope (chaps. 33—48). Editors seem to have underscored this transition by the motif of Ezekiel's dumbness. Seven days after the call of the prophet, Yahweh announced to him that he would be dumb and unable to reprove rebellious Israel (3:22-27). Later, God predicted that Ezekiel's mouth would be opened on the day a fugitive would bring him word of Jerusalem's fall (24:26-27). That promise came true in 33:22: "He had opened my mouth by the time the man came to me in the morning; so my mouth was opened, and I was no longer dumb." Clearly this does not mean that Ezekiel was silent during the first seven years of his ministry—chaps. 1—32 are full of his words.

---

4. Has the original date for the fourth vision (37:1-14) been lost? See Zimmerli, *Ezechiel*, p. 891. He suggests a date between 586/585 (33:21) and 571 (40:1) for the vision of the dry bones.

Rather, it is an editor's way of showing how after the fall of Jerusalem Ezekiel's mouth was opened to speak with boldness a great new word, a word of hope.[5]

GOD'S REAL PRESENCE IN BABYLON, HIS MOBILITY

The book begins with an account of the dazzling appearance of the likeness of the glory of Yahweh that knocked the prophet off his feet (chap. 1). Following this appearance Yahweh addressed Ezekiel and outlined to him his commission and the circumstances under which he would serve (2:1—3:15). Prototypes for such a call can be found in the calls of Micaiah ben Imlah (1 Kings 22:19–23) and Isaiah of Jerusalem (Isa. 6), but differences from these earlier accounts also abound. Tradition and innovation go hand in hand.

To some people today chap. 1 seems to be esoteric nonsense; to others it represents the account of a visit from outer space. The truth lies in another place. Almost all the details of this vision can be traced to ancient Near Eastern religiotheological culture,[6] or the idiom of theophanic descriptions in Israel. The intended effect of all the imagery: what Ezekiel saw there in Babylon was nothing else than Yahweh's own glory. That some details (e.g. the hands under the wings in v. 8) are not fully understandable and that the original picture of this chapter may have been supplemented by followers of Ezekiel are not to be denied.

The closer the text comes to describing the center of the theophany, the more words like *appearance* or *likeness* crop up (1:26–28). We would take this to be priestly reserve, a hesitancy to say that Ezekiel really saw God. In any case, the "man" he saw

---

5. Robert R. Wilson, "An Interpretation of Ezekiel's Dumbness," *VT* 22 (1972): 91–104, thinks the passages on Ezekiel's dumbness are attempts to defend him against the charge of failing to be a mediator for the people.

6. See the recent monograph by Othmar Keel, *Jahwe-Visionen und Siegelkunst*, Stuttgarter Bibel Studien 84/85 (Stuttgart: Katholisches Bibelwerk, 1977), pp. 125–273. Especially convincing is his interpretation of the four living creatures, vv. 5–6, as "heaven bearers." See pp. 207–16 and illustrations 156c–66, 180, and 182.

on the throne had an upper body that gleamed like bronze, a lower body that appeared to be made of fire. The lapis lazuli throne was set on a "firmament" (cf. Exod. 24:10), and below it were four animals, each having four heads and four wings and beside which there were wheels within wheels.[7] The whole conveyance could move easily in any direction and it was accompanied by a stormy wind, by the noise of an earthquake, Shaddai, "many waters," and by brightness of various sorts—images that are the common coin of theophanic descriptions in the Old Testament.

It was nothing short of the authentic glory of Yahweh that appeared to the prophet. We read, for example, of the heavens being opened and of Ezekiel seeing visions of God (v. 1). The animals who supported the throne had four wings and human features, not unlike the two-winged sphinxes that formed Yahweh's throne in the Solomonic temple. Their four heads represented the best of four categories of creatures: man, lion (king of the wild animals), the ox (supreme among domestic animals), and the eagle (the best of the birds)—only the finest could serve as this God's thronebearers.[8] The stormy wind that brought God's chariot throne came from the north, God's homeland in Israelite lore (Isa. 14:12; Ps. 48:2; Ezek. 38:6, 15; 39:2). The wheels were covered with eyes (v. 18), perhaps representing the all-seeingness or omnipresence of God.[9]

This glory appeared to the prophet, not in God's heavenly court (1 Kings 22), or even in Yahweh's heavenly/earthly temple (Isa. 6), but "among the exiles by the river Chebar" (1:1, 3). The throne appropriately was quite mobile: the animals that bore it had wings, legs, and even wheels! The spirit was its driving force

7. The wheels within wheels may come from a misunderstanding of thick, layered rims on certain depictions of wheels. See Keel, *Jahwe-Visionen*, pp. 263–67 and figs. 191–92.
8. Keel, *Jahwe-Visionen*, pp. 235–43 and 271, makes a convincing case for an alternate interpretation of the wings and faces. The four wings show that the beings incorporate four cosmic winds while the heads, based on Egyptian art, stand for the four compass points: lion (south), ox (north), eagle (east), and man (west).
9. Keel, *Jahwe-Visionen*, pp. 267–69, understands them as theological interpretations of nails driven into the rims of the wheels.

(v. 20). Because of the four animals, with their four heads and their wheels within wheels, the conveyance could take off in a new or different direction without turning (1:9, 12, 17). In short, a cascade of images declares Yahweh's mobility and his ability to be present in Babylon.

YAHWEH'S COMMISSIONING OF EZEKIEL

The commissioning speech which Ezekiel reports in chaps. 2— 3 initiated a most difficult ministry. The prophet was addressed by Yahweh as son of man, a title used here and ninety-two other times in Ezekiel to indicate the prophet's servant character and the great condescension of God to speak with him at all. In this title and in the emphasis on God's sending the prophet we find a testimony to Yahweh's sole responsibility for what happens to Israel, whether that be bad news or good.

Ezekiel's commission, in any case, was to bring very bad news. His audience included all of Israel, both northern and southern kingdoms, presumably also all Israel which had existed from the Exodus to the Exile. They all, "they and their fathers" (v. 3), had rebelled against Yahweh; they all were nothing but a house of rebels. The prophet was to match their hardness: his forehead would be like adamant harder than flint. Success was not to be his standard. Rather, he was to speak the word of Yahweh[10] regardless of whether they listened or not (2:5, 7; 3:11, 27).

He was literally to incorporate and personify his message. At Yahweh's direction he swallowed a scroll filled—on both sides!— with nothing but lamentation, mourning, and woe (2:10). He would speak to them, "Thus says Yahweh" (2:4), knowing that their rejection of him was finally and simply a rejection of Yahweh himself (3:7). This bitter word tasted like honey to Ezekiel, not because he was masochistic (he was only one who had been sent) but because it was the word of Yahweh (cf. Jer. 15:16). By definition Yahweh's words are a joy and a delight.

God's actions, in judgment or grace, are never the final word in Ezekiel. Rather, Yahweh's actions are to enable Israel or the

10. The expression "the word of Yahweh came to me/to Ezekiel" occurs more than forty times in the book.

nations to know and acknowledge the God who revealed himself in the simple self-proclamation, "I am Yahweh." Such "words of demonstration" occur nearly eighty times in Ezekiel.[11] They come as the conclusion of words against the land of Israel (e.g. 7:2–4), at the end of oracles against foreign nations (e.g. 25: 3–5), and at the end of words of salvation (e.g. 37:6, 13, 14). Judging Israel and the nations or delivering Israel is only God's penultimate goal. However hard Ezekiel's message was from 593–587, it beat to the drums of God's love. Ezekiel's prophetic ministry was to help Israel recognize that God's prophet had been among them (2:5; cf. 33:33). To know this fact and to acknowledge the Lord who stands behind the prophet mean finally to confess the deeds of him who "says it all" in the words "I am Yahweh." Ezekiel's no to Israel demonstrated God's faithfulness, but his hard no was also in the service of God's ultimate yes. God's fidelity allowed no ignoring of Israel's rebellion, but Ezekiel's God was both faithful and free: he had wrath but he was not limited to it. In words from the Book of Ezekiel: "They [Israel] shall know that I am Yahweh their God because I sent them into exile among the nations, and then gathered them into their own land" (39:28; cf. 17:24).

LAMENTATION, MOURNING, AND WOE: GOD'S NO TO ISRAEL

For the first six years of his exilic ministry Ezekiel had to announce a final no to Israel's history. That itself is an important voice from exile. False prophets might fail to step into the breach, or they might plaster over the troubles with cries of "Peace, peace," even when there was no peace (13:1–16), but Ezekiel, himself an exile, affirmed the finality and the correctness of God's judgment. In his view there was no way around 587, either militarily or theologically.

11. Walther Zimmerli has traced the history of this expression in earlier biblical literature and its function in the book of Ezekiel itself. See "Ich bin Jahwe," "Erkenntnis Gottes nach dem Buche Ezechiel," and "Das Wort des göttlichen Selbsterweises (Erweiswort), eine prophetische Gattung," *Gottes Offenbarung*, pp. 11–40, 41–119, 120–32. See nn. 5–9 on p. 43 for a list of the biblical passages involved.

"The end has come" is the way he put it in chap. 7. Aye, "the day of the wrath of Yahweh comes." The themes of Yahweh's day and of the end had been employed already by his predecessor Amos (5:18; 8:2) in the eighth century, but two factors made Ezekiel's no to Israel especially difficult:

a. A group existed in Jerusalem who thought the bottom had already been hit by the first deportation in 597. Having weathered that storm, they were ready to claim possession of the land, perhaps even to begin a rebuilding program (11:3). They reacted to God's judgment with opportunistic resignation: "Life has its ups and downs. The deportation of the ruling classes is our lucky break. Why, we already outnumber Abraham, that single man who nevertheless acquired land" (11:15; 33:24).

b. Secondly, Ezekiel's no was spoken to Jerusalem, God's chosen city. This prophet was after all a priest, and he proclaimed his message among a people who sang, "If I forget you, O Jerusalem, let my right hand wither!" (Ps. 137:5). Yet his vision of the abominations in the temple (chap. 8) ended with an uncompromising, heartrending sight: six executioners were dispatched through the city to kill both old and young, not excluding women and children (9:6). Though some people were marked out for deliverance by a *taw* marked on their foreheads (9:4), the size of the destruction forced Ezekiel to cry out for a halt (9:8). Instead, the destruction moved from the people to the burning of the city and then to the departure of Yahweh's glory from the temple. On a vehicle not unlike the chariot throne of chap. 1, the glory moved to the threshold of the temple, then on to its east gate (10:19), and finally to the Mount of Olives (11:23). One senses in this hesitant departure a grieving over the destruction it symbolized.

THE SIGN ACTIONS:
ANTICIPATIONS OF JUDGMENT

Ezekiel's well-known, often esoteric sign actions also proclaimed the fate of Jerusalem. What he experienced in them anticipated what God's word was about to do against Jerusalem. The siege he acted out against a model of Jerusalem drawn on a brick was neither a war game nor a sign of the prophet's disturbed mental condition: it was a prediction of things to come (4:1–3). He also acted out a life under siege rations when he scraped together a few grains from the bottom of the barrel in order to stay alive (4:9, 10a), and he used his own hair to dramatize how Jerusalem's inhabitants would be burned in the city, killed in flight, or driven into exile (5:1–2). His orders were to march into exile with a pack on his back (12:1–16), eat his bread with quaking and dismay over the coming stripping of Jerusalem (12:17–20), or sigh with broken heart over the latest news from the homeland (21:6–7). He was ordered to set up a signpost pointing to Rabbah of the Ammonites and Judah-Jerusalem, two alternate routes of attack for the sword of Nebuchadnezzar. When the king's divination procedures would lead him to attack Jerusalem first (21:18–23), he would hurry to carry out the divine sentence on a city legally convicted of sin. Even the death of Ezekiel's wife was an occasion for proclamation: the prophet was forbidden to mourn for her. When asked the reason for his tearless reaction to the loss of his eye's delight, he pointed once more to the imminent destruction of the temple. The people would not mourn or weep for that either, he observed, but they would pine away in their iniquities (24:23).

WHY MUST THE END COME?

The offenses of Israel were omnipresent and wide-ranging in Ezekiel's telling. The reader grows weary of the endless recounting of words like abominations (tô'ēbôt), detestable things (šiqqûṣîm), idols (gillûlîm) and harlotries (taznûtîm). Nevertheless, we need to survey some of the key indictments Ezekiel leveled against his contemporaries in order to understand the seriousness of the Exile in the prophet's eyes.

a. Ezekiel 6. The mountains of Israel are here castigated for their high places, regular altars, incense altars, idols, and their sanctuaries on every high hill and under every green tree and leafy oak. The vocabulary recalls that of the Deuteronomic reform. It would seem that the reform lost its effectiveness after Josiah's death and that under Jehoiakim many of the old syncretistic practices returned.

b. Ezekiel 8. In a great vision Ezekiel visited the temple in

Jerusalem and observed four of its abominations. Many of the details remain unclear, but he seems to have seen: (1) an altar outside the temple itself (an explicit violation of Deuteronomy's law of centralization), which threatened to drive Yahweh far from his sanctuary (8:3, 5–6); (2) a secret rite in a dark room, perhaps representing the cult of the dead, associated with Osiris (8:7–13);[12] (3) women weeping for the Sumero-Babylonian vegetation deity Tammuz or Dumuzi (8:14–15); (4) twenty-five men worshiping the sun right at the door of the temple.

Jeremiah mentions no such abominations in the post-Josian temple. Did Ezekiel base his critique on the sins actually being committed in his day, or has he selected sins from various eras of Israel's history to characterize their utter rejection of God? Such a telescoping of Israel's sin history might account for his catalog of sins in chap. 6 as well.

c. Ezekiel 15. The only specific offense mentioned in this chapter is Israel's faithless actions (v. 8). More important is the way in which Ezekiel characterizes the people as lacking any worth. He compares them to the "wood" of a grapevine which has no value for the carpenter even when it is whole. How much less when it is burned and charred! Israel's general claim to value before God is denied; its specific status after the first deportation of 597 is only that of potential fuel for more fire.

d. Ezekiel 16 and 23. These chapters compare Jerusalem's or Israel's behavior to that of adulterous women (cf. Hos. 1—3; Jer. 2:2–3; 3:6–14). According to chap. 16, Jerusalem was bad from the beginning. Her father was an Amorite, her mother a Hittite, apparently the prophet's theological interpretation of the city's late incorporation into Israel. Despite Yahweh's loving care, Jerusalem played the harlot, both by consorting with other gods and, at least according to the present text, by associating with other nations—Egypt, Philistia, Assyria, and Chaldea. Jerusalem is a harlot who pays her customers, an ironic allusion to the tribute she had dispatched to foreign powers. Jerusalem is worse than

12. Cf. W. F. Albright, *Archaeology and the Religion of Israel* (Baltimore: Johns Hopkins, 1953), pp. 166–67.

Samaria, which fell in 721; aye, she is worse even than Sodom, whose people failed to help the poor and needy. In comparison with Jerusalem, Samaria and Sodom appear righteous!

Chap. 23 continues the accusation of spiritual harlotry, but now it is used to describe two sisters, Oholah and Oholibah, standing respectively for Samaria and Jerusalem, the capitals of the northern and southern kingdoms. The southern kingdom is depicted as being much worse than the northern, especially in her running from one foreign lover (ally) to another. She flitted from the Assyrians (vv. 12–13) to the Babylonians (vv. 14–18), only to pick up with the Egyptians (vv. 19–21). Behind this last accusation we should see a criticism of Jerusalem's vain alliances with Egypt in her final days. Such harlotry, says Ezekiel, is what she did in Egypt already before the Exodus.

e. Ezekiel 20. In response to an inquiry brought by the elders of Israel before the final fall of Jerusalem, Ezekiel told a negative "salvation history" in three phases that fully justified Yahweh's brusque rejection of the inquiry in v. 31. Israel had benefited from God's gracious acts and received instructions or laws from God in each of the three phases, but she acted rebelliously against him and called forth his wrath. Nevertheless, Yahweh acted repeatedly for the sake of his name, lest it be profaned among the nations, and he did not pour out his wrath.

The cause for all these severe judgments is solely Israel's Neither the period in Egypt nor the one in the wilderness (per contra Hosea and Jeremiah) was the "good old days." Israel was rebellious right from the start in Egypt. There never had been a time of faithfulness. So deeply rooted is the people's sin that their behavior in the land is irrelevant—one way or the other—to the question of the onrushing judgment.[13] Since the present generation doggedly repeats the sins of the fathers, their inquiry is rejected outright.

Why must the end come? Despite his long and at times verbose telling of Israel's faults (cf. also 22:1–16, 23–31), Ezekiel seems

13. The history of Israel in the land, vv. 27–29, is the contribution of a later hand.

to be at a distance from the day-to-day events of Jerusalem's last six years. We have no sure way of telling how many of the specific charges are plausible, but his main point was that the guilt for all of Israel's history would come to a head in the present generation. Israel's history lacked any period in which righteousness prevailed. From the stay in Egypt until his own day, the prophet sees nothing but abominations, detestable things, idols, and harlotry.

JUDGMENT ON THE NATIONS

The Book of Ezekiel contains words against seven nations in chaps. 25—32, and a further oracle against Edom in chap. 35. Despite disagreements, now as before, over which of these oracles comes from the prophet himself, a number of observations can be made on the present text that help us understand Israel's reaction to exile. It is doubtful that any of these oracles can be dated later than the sixth century.

1. Tyre is rebuked for its pride (28:1–10), especially for its pride in its beauty (27:3; 28:17); for its violence (28:16); and for the unrighteousness of its trade (28:18). The prophet also scores Tyre for rejoicing over Jerusalem's fall (26:2).

2. Ammon, Moab, Edom, and Philistia are similarly criticized for celebrating the profanation of God's sanctuary and the fall of Judah, and for sharing in the plundering of the land. The judgment on Israel had stemmed from God's righteous decision; it should not be the occasion for self-aggrandizement or territorial expansion by others.

3. The oracles against Egypt criticize it for its useless offers of support for Judah in the final years and for the disastrous false trust this evoked from Israel (29:6–7). Egypt's pride (29:3, 9), its arrogance as a superpower (31:3ff.), and its violence (32:32) have earned it total annihilation at the hands of Babylon.

4. The word of demonstration form (*Erweiswort*) abounds in the oracles against the nations. Thus, the punishment of the nations is seen not as an end in itself or even merely as retribution for the sins mentioned in paragraphs 2–3 above. Rather, the

seven foreign nations will come to know and acknowledge through their experiences of judgment the God who says "I am Yahweh." Such an acknowledgment by the nations is the goal also of God's *saving acts* for Israel (e.g. Ezek. 36:23; 37:28).

5. The destruction of the nations is the beginning of Israel's salvation. No longer will these nations hurt Israel (28:24). Their defeat, in fact, will be followed by Israel's renewed dwelling in the land (28:25) or the exaltation of Israel's power (= its horn, 29:21). Through the events connected with the defeat of the nations, Israel too "will know that I am Yahweh" (e.g. 28:24, 26).

A NEW EXODUS: GOD'S YES TO ISRAEL

Like the D redaction of Jeremiah and like Second Isaiah, Ezekiel foresaw a new exodus as God's way of remaining faithful to the promise inherent in the first exodus. The most extensive treatment of this motif appears in a disputation word at 20:32–44 that has been placed at the end of the pericope rejecting the elders' inquiry (20:1–31).[14] The passage begins with the people's expression of defeat and hopelessness. If God's judgment is inescapable since his decision on exile had been reached before Israel entered the land under Joshua, why not live among the nations in peace and serve their idols (v. 32)? Yahweh replied with an oath: "As I live, says Lord Yahweh, surely with a mighty hand and an outstretched arm, and with wrath poured out, I will be king over you. I will bring you out from the peoples and gather you out of the countries where you are scattered" (vv. 33–34).

God's kingship meant that he would bring a new exodus (cf. Exod. 15:18), surely a promise that was not easily believable early in the Exile. Yahweh had to argue for it by invoking a curse on himself ("as I live . . ."). His kingship could be inaugurated only by a power display against the enemy. In addition, his wrath would be poured out, according to Ezekiel, on the rebels and transgressors within exilic Israel (v. 38; cf. v. 8, 13, 21). That is,

14. See Zimmerli, "Der 'neue Exodus' in der Verkündigung der beiden grossen Exilspropheten," *Gottes Offenbarung,* pp. 192–204. Cf. Baltzer, *Ezechiel und Deuterojesaja,* pp. 2–11.

not everyone who would experience the new exodus would be allowed to go on to Zion. Instead, the exodus would commence from many countries (v. 34), and it would lead to a judgmental confrontation between Yahweh and Israel in the "wilderness of the peoples" (v. 35). Yahweh would be Israel's judge (v. 36) as he had judged and purified Israel during its first desert wandering. Like a shepherd he would make all sheep pass under his staff, with the result that only a few and then only those who did not rebel or transgress (v. 38) would enter the land of Israel (cf. 34: 17–19 and Matt. 25:31–46).

The goal of this new exodus is a procession to Zion, not merely a retaking of the land (v. 40). Attainment of this goal will demonstrate God's holiness, his godhead, for all the nations to see (v. 41). The gift of the land itself (v. 42; cf. 11:17–18; 34:13; 36:24; 37:21) will be the fulfillment of the old promise to the fathers, and it will lead to a double insight: (1) the people will know and acknowledge that their God is that Yahweh whose identity was disclosed at the time of the first exodus (v. 42: cf. Exod. 3 and 6); and (2) they will be led to recognize their own shameful behavior when they see the great deeds of God's kindness (v. 43).[15] The only reason why exilic Israel can know God is that Yahweh acts for his own name's sake and not according to their own corrupt doings (v. 44). That name, or reputation, was slandered when Israel went into captivity among the nations (36:22). Now Yahweh must save his own reputation—that is, he must vindicate his holiness—by rescuing Israel (36:23; cf. 39:25). Israel's miserable condition is *not* the reason why Yahweh chooses to act (36:22–23).

In sum, the new exodus for Ezekiel presents the faithful God acting freely, that is, in a way appropriate to the new situation of exile. The prophet's stern picture of God as king, judge, and shepherd reminded his contemporaries of their accountability for the Exile's judgment. Yet Ezekiel's Yahweh also counteracts

---

15. Cf. 6:8–10; 16:54, 62–63. Similarly, the new temple will make Israel remember with shame her former iniquities (43:10–11).

the despair of the people by promising military action against their foes and by invoking self-imprecations to support his own words. By manifesting his holiness Yahweh will produce a purified remnant as a witness to the nations. On his holy mountain, toward which the exiles freed from Babylon process, Yahweh will accept his repentant people and receive from them their faithful and abundant offerings.

THE GOOD SHEPHERD

Chap. 34 begins with a woe oracle against the shepherds or rulers of Israel, who have only cared for themselves and not for the flock (people) entrusted to them. They have not fed the sheep, strengthened the weak, healed the sick, bound up the crippled, brought back the strayed, or sought the lost. Ruling violently, they turned their flock over to wild beasts. The unrighteous rulers, in short, are responsible for Israel's falling prey to the nations. The bottom line on this unit is a word of judgment against these rulers or shepherds (v. 10; cf. 17:11–21; 19:1–9, 10–14; 21:25–27).

Yet the chapter goes on to describe how Yahweh himself will act as the good shepherd. He will seek out the lost sheep in exile and will bring them home to Palestine where he will feed the hungry and help all who are injured or oppressed. Later traditionalists (see especially vv. 23–24) modified this word by having Yahweh promise to rule through an *earthly* shepherd, a new David. The monergism of God's action as shepherd presupposed in the original oracle, however, is the real strength of Ezekiel's own solution to the problem of exile.

CREATION AND RESURRECTION

The theocentric emphasis is also well represented in the vision of the dry bones (37:1–14). In this vision the prophet saw a valley covered with bones that were both numerous and dry. This symbolism meant that many people had died and that they had been dead for a long time. Ezekiel was told to prophesy to these bones and tell them that Yahweh would supply them with sinews, flesh, and skin, and that then he would enliven them by giving them breath (v. 6). Clearly, the prophet understands the resurrection of these bones as a new creation; the parallels to J's creation account (Gen. 2:7; cf. Eccles. 12:7) are unmistakable. A great theophanic noise accompanies the reassembly of the bones, and the enlivening spirit comes, at the prophet's invitation, to set the re-formed people on their feet as a mighty army. This vision is interpreted by vv. 11–14. The interpretation identified the bones with the whole house of Israel and cites three complaints of the people, which are then disputed: "Our bones are dried up, and our hope is lost; we are clean cut off" (v. 11). Strangely, the metaphor soon changes from bones strewn on a battlefield to corpses lying in graves. While the metaphor in vv. 1–10 was primarily that of new creation, the miracle described in vv. 11–14 is more explicitly resurrection. In addition, the verb employed for "bringing up" from the graves is used elsewhere in the Bible to denote the Exodus (1 Sam. 12:6; Hos. 12:14). This resurrection/exodus is to be followed by life in the land.

Several observations seem warranted:

1. Radical dependency on God for any future hope is the major theme of this passage. The very dryness of the bones and the people's complaints about their hopeless condition emphasize that no self-deliverance is possible. By describing the restoration of Israel as a creation, resurrection, exodus, or a new gift of the land, the prophet alludes to activities which by definition are solely the work of God. Furthermore, the "breath" is not merely the breath of life related in some way to the four winds (v. 9). It is the spirit that comes from Yahweh—"my spirit" (v. 14).

2. New life in the land is not an end in itself. Rather, the enlivening of the enfleshed bones (v. 6) or the resurrection and subsequent gift of the land (vv. 13–14) have as their ultimate intention Israel's recognition and acknowledgment of Yahweh's true identity: "You shall know that I am Yahweh." This faith goal, this doxological intention, puts decisive checks on any merely nationalist understanding of salvation.

3. The pericope ends with a powerful appeal to the word of

God as the basis for hope: "I have spoken and I will do it, oracle of Yahweh" (v. 14, RWK). The hope conveyed by this vision is not just a possibility, one of many future scenarios. Israel can count on it, it is part of God's word. The power that guarantees new life after exile is that creative word of God proclaimed by the prophet.

A future for Israel can only be understood under the category of life from death. The radicality of judgment and the radicality of God's salvation could hardly be more sharply expressed. Israel's misery is not just its fate; it is also its guilt. Israel's future will happen without any self-help on her part. The vision of the dry bones expresses God's unconditional promise for the future (but see 18:24).

THE SPECIFICS OF THE NEW AGE:
A NEW COVENANT

In passages thought to be authentic Ezekiel does not frequently or unambiguously use the term *covenant* to describe preexilic Israel's relationship to Yahweh. His picture of future Israel, however, includes an everlasting covenant of peace, and in this idea he shows both continuity and contrast with other exilic authors.

1. 34:25–30.[16] The new covenant described in these verses is called a covenant of peace, a promise of wholeness and prosperity. Wild animals will no longer disturb Israel (vv. 25, 28; cf. v. 8),[17] nor will enemy nations oppress, enslave, or reproach them (vv. 27–29). In fact, Israel will dwell securely in the wilderness and sleep in the woods (vv. 25 and 27), and no one will intimidate them (v. 28). The covenantal peace will mean good rainfall, fruitful trees, abundant crops, and an end of hunger (vv. 26, 27, 29; cf. 36:29–30, 34–35). A word of demonstration containing the covenant formula brings this pericope to its climax: "They shall

16. This passage is one of a series of supplements to the description of Yahweh as good shepherd in vv. 1–16. While the words may come from the school of Ezekiel rather than from the prophet himself, they are hardly to be dated later than the end of the Exile. Cf. Zimmerli, *Ezechiel*, p. 847.

17. Elsewhere in Ezekiel wild animals are agents of God's punishment (5:17; 14:15, 21; 33:27).

know that I, Yahweh their God, am with them, and that they, the house of Israel, are my people" (v. 30). The detailed blessings of this new covenant display many verbal similarities to Lev. 26:3–13, but the blessings according to Leviticus are responses to human obedience; in Ezekiel's monergistic theology they are free gifts of God. No reference is made in Ezekiel to any specific agricultural efforts; everything comes from Yahweh's hand.

2. 37:26. "I will make with them a covenant of peace, an eternal covenant it will be, and I will multiply them."[18] Two comments need to be made on this passage. First, the new covenant includes the blessing of human fertility—good news for a people in exile and similar to the command/promise to be fruitful and multiply which we will study in P (chap. 6). Great population growth is also promised in 36:10–11, 33, 36, 37–38, where we read also of the restoration and rebuilding of the cities (cf. 28:26). Secondly, the covenant, though everlasting and connected with fertility as in P, is a new covenant, even if the word *new* is not explicitly used. Ezekiel does not rely on the covenants with Noah or Abraham (like P) or appeal to a return to Horeb/Sinai (like Deuteronomy; cf. Dtr). The new covenant he foretells has many similarities with the new or renewed Sinai covenant referred to in Jeremiah (31:31–34).

3. 16:59–63.[19] In this pericope Yahweh confirms that Jerusalem has broken the covenant and will experience punishment appropriate to her deeds. Yet, he promises to remember the earlier covenant (v. 60; cf. v. 8) made in the days of her youth, despite the fact that Jerusalem has persistently forgotten her faithful youth (vv. 22 and 43). When Yahweh remembers, he will establish an everlasting covenant, leading Jerusalem to know and acknowledge him.

The giving of this covenant is linked with the forgiveness of

18. For the text see *BHS* and Zimmerli, *Ezechiel*, p. 906.

19. Vv. 44–58 deal with Jerusalem and her sisters rather than with Jerusalem herself as in vv. 1–43. Since vv. 59–63 build on vv. 44–58, they are not part of the original text, though there is no need to date them later than the end of the Exile.

sins, as in Jeremiah (v. 63). Since the broken covenant carried with it God's curse, the promise of a new covenant might seem to trivialize God's anger or make him appear inconsistent. Ezekiel, however, affirms the full depth of Israel's sin and holds to the necessity of God's punishment. A new covenant is only possible theologically and logically by the interposition of God's gracious forgiveness. Forgiveness also plays a role in Yahweh's promise to purify restored Israel: "I will sprinkle clean water upon you, and you shall be clean from all your uncleannesses, and from all your idols I will cleanse you" (36:25; cf. v. 33).

The new covenant will last forever. The corollary of this permanence is that the Israel of the restoration will be faithful and obedient. God will enable Israel's new obedience by inwardly transforming them: "A new heart I will give you, and a new spirit I will put within you; and I will take out of your flesh the heart of stone and give you a heart of flesh. And I will put my spirit within you, and cause you to walk in my statutes and be careful to observe my ordinances" (36:26–27; cf. v. 29 and 11:19). Only Yahweh's actions and his forgiveness free Israel for service (cf. 34:22; 37:23).

The new covenant is part of God's faithfulness to his earlier relationship with Israel, but it is also part of his gracious freedom in that (a) the covenant is made possible by his forgiveness, (b) it will result in a faithful Israel, and (c) it will last forever.

ONE NATION, ONE PRINCE-KING

Could there be an Israel without a Davidic king? Ezekiel had much to say against earlier princes of Israel (cf. 22:6, 25) and especially against Zedekiah, the last king (17:12ff.), but the promise to David remained for him, or at least for the members of his school who edited his work, part of the ongoing fidelity of Yahweh. Yet, Yahweh was free to modify the description and function of the royal office. The Book of Ezekiel includes restrictions on the future royal office, thus offering an implicit criticism of previous excesses, and gives it a far lesser role than the notion of the "presence of God" which is at the center of the prophet's picture of coming times.[20] Though almost all the passages dealing with the future Davidide may be supplements to authentic oracles, none of them presupposes the later difficulties connected with the disappearance of Zerubbabel. A date between 587 and 538—that is, in the Exile—seems probable for all of the following items.[21]

1. 17:22–24. In this supplement to vv. 1–21, Yahweh promises to take a piece from the top of the cedar and plant it on the high mountain of Israel. The cedar stands for the Davidic line, the high mountain for Zion. From this new tender plant will grow a gigantic tree in which all the creatures of the earth, both beasts and birds, will seek refuge. No specifics are given about the character of this coming ruler, nor are we informed about any of his activities. The whole point seems to be that all the trees of the field, that is, all nations, will recognize in this new act Yahweh at his characteristic best; he humbles the proud and exalts the lowly (cf. 1 Sam. 2:7; cf. Luke 2:52). The new monarch of the Davidic line will not inaugurate the new age by military strength. Rather, Yahweh alone brings new times whose peaceful character will redound to his own glory. The promise, in any case, is sure: "I have spoken and I will do it" (v. 24).

2. 34:23–24. This messianic supplement promises that alongside Yahweh the good shepherd (vv. 11–16) there will be *one* earthly shepherd. The emphasis on the word *one* shows that the divided kingdom with its attendant evils will be a thing of the past. The new shepherd is to be called "my servant" and "David." Earlier prophets had identified the Messiah as a descendant of David (Isa. 9:6–7; Jer. 23:5–6), and the use of the title David for him is not unknown elsewhere (Hos. 3:5; Jer. 30:9–10). Yahweh explicates his relationship to the messiah in a modified covenant formula: "I Yahweh will be God for them; my servant David will be prince in their midst." The title *prince* may be an

20. God's gift of a new king/prince is never the rationale behind a word of demonstration, thus showing its less-than-central significance.

21. Cf. Zimmerli, *Ezechiel*, p. 1248. None of the words about the *nāśi'* in Ezek. 40—48 can be dated *prior* to 571.

attempt to show the ancient roots of this office in Israel (cf. Exod. 22:7), or it may be an implicit criticism of the pretensions of or the corruption of preexilic kingship.

3. 37:22 and 24–28. After the vision of the valley of dry bones (vv. 1–14), chap. 37 contains an account of a symbolic act, promising the reunification of Israel (vv. 15–19). Israel's future is not to be plagued with the troubles of the divided kingdom. A supplement to this symbolic act in vv. 20–23 (24a) makes the reunification a product of the new exodus and the new gift of the land. Just as there would no longer be two kingdoms, so there would no longer be two kings. The promise of one king in v. 22 is only the corollary of a reunited Israel.

In the following pericope, vv. 24b–28, we are told of new Israel's obedience, and this is followed by four promises that will be everlasting—the land, the Davidic prince, the covenant, and God's presence in the sanctuary. As we shall see, the last of these is of climactic importance. As to the Davidic prince who will last forever, it is important to note that his presence is almost incidental, and nothing specific is said about his function.

4. 40—48. In these final chapters of Ezekiel reference to a prince (*nāśî'*) is made some twenty times, though perhaps none of these references comes from the original draft of the book. The prince will receive land (45:7; 48:21, 22) on either side of the territory assigned to the priests and Levites and on either side of the city (see diagram below). This will guarantee him income, but it is also meant as a polemic: never again will the kings appropriate the property of average citizens (45:8), an offense which the Deuteronomist had already seen as an ever-present danger (1 Sam. 8:11–17a). This royal land will be inviolable (46:16–18), but by the same token the prince will not be able to violate the land of others under this arrangement.

In addition to land, the prince will receive certain taxes (45:16) from which he is to provide the offerings for various feasts including the Passover (45:17, 22). The prince will perform his cultic duties in the east gate (44:3; 46:1–12) as a first among equals. He will be the most prominent member of the worshiping community, but a member of the community nevertheless, without explicit priestly functions. No rulership functions are assigned to him in 40—48.

THE LAND

Though Ezekiel contains little or nothing about a new conquest, the promise of the land frequently appears. By giving the land once more to Israel, Yahweh will remain faithful to his promises to the patriarchs, especially to Jacob (20:42; 28:25; 37:25; 47:14). The land will be considered permanent just like the covenant and kingship. A broken covenant had led to loss of land and resultant exile. In the new, unbreakable possession of the land, no one will be able to make Israel afraid (e.g. 34:28), and the people will dwell on the land securely (e.g. 34:25). The promise of the land is made concrete in the descriptions of its extent and of its divisions (45:1–8; 47:13—48:29).[22] Ezekiel's placing of the eastern border along the Jordan River (47:18) may reflect the fact that the Transjordanian territories throughout their history had been more open to the suspicion of syncretism, idolatry, and apostasy. Excluding these territories from the promised land lessens the risk of any future falling-away.

The map's division into twelve tribal allotments and a central sacred area symbolizes God's saving intent; it is not a realistic blueprint. No irregularities of geography are taken into account in drawing the tribal boundaries, but each tribe is ascribed an equal portion (47:14). Perhaps we should see here a reaffirmation of the egalitarian principles of early Israel, according to which all things really belong to Yahweh and no one was to accumulate riches at the expense of his neighbor (Lev. 25:13, 23; cf. also Isa. 5:8 and Mic. 2:1–5). The reinstitution of the tribal divisions may be implicit criticism of Solomon, whose new administrative

---

22. These sections come from later, though still exilic, hands. For detailed discussion see G. Ch. Macholz, "Noch Einmal: Planungen für den Wiederaufbau nach der Katastrophe von 587," *VT* 19 (1969) : 322–52; W. Zimmerli, "Planungen für den Wiederaufbau nach der Katastrophe von 587," *VT* 18 (1968) : 229–55; and idem, "Ezechieltempel und Salomostadt," *Hebräische Wortforschung* VTSup 16 (1967) : 398–414.

districts dispensed with the old tribal system (1 Kings 4:7-19). The map of the new land of Israel can be diagramed as follows:

Dan (Bilhah-Rachel)   Eastern Boundary =
Asher (Zilpah-Leah)   Jordan River
Naphtali (Bilhah-Rachel)
Manasseh* (Rachel)
Ephraim* (Rachel)
Reuben* (Leah)
Judah* (Leah)

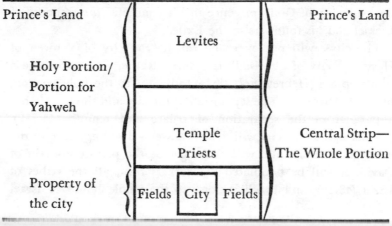

Prince's Land   Prince's Land
                           Levites

Holy Portion/
Portion for
Yahweh
                          Temple   Central Strip—
                          Priests   The Whole Portion

Property of   Fields City Fields
the city

Benjamin* (Rachel)
Simeon* (Leah)
Issachar* (Leah)
Zebulun* (Leah)
Gad (Zilpah-Leah)

We note that Dan is still in the north, as in preexilic times (Judg. 18:27; but cf. Josh. 19:40–48), and that seven of the twelve tribes are north of the central strip, thus approximating the greater size of the territory once known as the northern kingdom. In general, however, the organizing principle is quite different from the original land division. The land of Israel now finds its focus on the central strip within which are portions for the Levites, the priests, and the city. Within the priests' portion is the temple with its guarantee of God's presence (see below). Next to the central strip, to both north and south, are four tribes that we have marked with an asterisk. What they have in common is that these "sons of Jacob" were born to one of the patriarch's full wives, Leah or Rachel. The other four sons resulted from the union of Jacob with Bilhah or Zilpah, his wives' maids. Degrees of holiness are laid out: first the central strip with the temple, then the territories of the "full-born" sons, then those of the sons of the concubines. Thus, the whole land offers silent testimony to the centrality of God's presence in his temple as *the* response of Ezekiel and his followers to the Exile.

The city[23] will no longer be called "the city of Yahweh of Hosts, the city of our God" (Ps. 48:8). Rather, it has become a secular place (Hebrew *ḥōl,* 48:15), adjacent to the holy portion, but not a part of it. The separation of the city and the temple has a parallel in the separation of palace and temple (43:7–9). Neither palace nor city will defile Yahweh's dwelling place in the new age. The city also will no longer be the private domain of David. It will be populated by workers from all the tribes of Israel (48:19), and it will belong to the whole house of Israel (45:6).

YAHWEH IS THERE

All the hopes of Ezekiel for the future culminate in and focus on the everlasting presence of God with his people. A paragraph in chap. 37 (vv. 25–28) sets out the promise in dramatic fashion: (1) An obedient Israel will dwell in the land for ever. (2) David will be prince forever. (3) Yahweh will give the people a covenant that lasts forever. (4) "I will set my sanctuary in their midst for ever. My dwelling place shall be with them; and I will be their God and they shall be my people. Then the nations shall know

---

23. Obviously Jerusalem is intended, though the name itself is not used in 48:15–19.

that I Yahweh sanctify Israel, when my sanctuary is in the midst of them for ever." The promise that Yahweh will dwell in the midst of his people is stated three times; twice it is underscored with the term *for ever*. Only this promise is connected with the covenant formula ("I will be their God and they shall be my people"). Only the fulfillment of this promise will cause the nations to acknowledge Yahweh.

Chaps. 40—42 contain Ezekiel's vision of the new temple.[24] In the twenty-fifth year of his exile,[25] Ezekiel was brought to the land of Israel and was set down on a high mountain (40:2). Ezekiel saw three outer gates, located on the east, north, and south respectively, leading into the outer courtyard. Facing these gates were three more gates leading to the inner court (40:1–37). The architectural prototype of these gates has been discovered by modern archaeologists in tenth-century Solomonic contexts at Gezer, Megiddo, and Hazor. Presumably, Jerusalem also itself had such gates (cf. 1 Kings 9:15, 19). In any case, Ezekiel has transferred these gates from the city defenses to the temple area itself. Since there is no western gate, we might suppose that the prophet meant to render impossible the sin of 8:16–18. However one approached the new temple, he would not face the rising sun in the east.

Ezekiel was subsequently led through the inner court into the temple itself, which was divided into a vestibule, a nave, and an inner room. At this latter place, where God would dwell, Ezekiel's visionary companion exclaimed, "This is the most holy place" (40:47—41:4). The "original" vision concluded with the measuring of the entire temple complex (42:15–20).

At this point Ezekiel was brought back to the east gate, where he saw and heard the glory of God returning from the east, from the Babylonian Exile. This was the same glory that had appeared

24. Perhaps only 40:1–37; 40:47—41:4; and 42:15–20 are to be considered original. So Wevers; cf. Zimmerli.
25. Zimmerli notes that the dimensions of the buildings in the temple vision are all multiples of twenty-five. He suggests that this number twenty-five reflects the twenty-fifth year of the date formula and that the twenty-fifth year would make the halfway point of a jubilee period when a release could be expected.

at his call (chaps. 1—3) and at his vision of Jerusalem's destruction (chaps. 8—11). This glory reentered through the east gate and filled the temple (43:1–5). The east gate, through which the glory had passed, was then permanently closed (44:1–2). No one would ever again step on the holy path by which Yahweh had returned. With the gate permanently closed, Yahweh's presence could also be considered permanent.

What would God's presence mean for Israel? Ezekiel's guide took him back to the door of the temple, and there he saw water flowing from the temple toward the east. At first it was only ankle deep, but it grew gradually deeper until one could only swim in it; it had become too deep for walking (47:1–6). Along the banks of this river were trees which bore fresh fruit every month. When the river emptied into the Dead Sea it made the briny waters fresh, and fish abounded even in the (formerly) Dead Sea (47:7–12). The meaning of this passage becomes clear when it is studied against the background of ancient Near Eastern and Old Testament tradition. The Canaanite god El had his dwelling at the meeting place of two rivers, and the Old Testament also frequently associates water with Yahweh's dwelling place (Gen. 2:10–14; Ps. 46:4; cf. Isa. 8:5–8). Hence, Ezekiel's description of a stream at God's dwelling place is in itself no surprise. But his stream represents also the marvelous transforming powers of God's presence: it brings to life the infertile Judean wilderness and even gives life to that sea whose very name is the epitome of all lifelessness. God's presence, in short, brings about a new creation of the land. When later hands added the description of the extent and divisions of the land in 47:13—48:29, they described a land that was healed by God's presence. All former dangers and iniquities were done away by God's presence: its zones of holiness pointed to the importance of God's temple presence with a kind of silent praise.

Whoever was responsible for the final pericope in the book (48:30–35) also wanted to testify to the importance of God's presence. He differed from the tradents responsible for the land division pericope (47:13—48:29) in that the twelve tribal names he gave to Jerusalem's gates included the tribe of Levi and consequently combined Ephraim and Manasseh in their father

Joseph. He differed from Ezekiel in that he restored Jerusalem itself to its old religious importance as the dwelling place of God, but he echoed Ezekiel's own theological response to exile when he wrote, "And the name of that city henceforth shall be, 'Yahweh is there'" (48:35). The city's name proclaims the heartbeat of this priestly-prophetic theology. God's presence legitimated Ezekiel's call and provided a measure of comfort for the exiles themselves (11:16). God's reentry and permanent dwelling in the midst of the people would take place only by virtue of his own gracious decision—and it would make all things new and alive.

CALLED TO BE A WATCHMAN

The Book of Ezekiel contains a second call of the prophet (3:16b–21; 33:1–9) in which he is assigned the dangerous task of watchman: He is to warn people about their wickedness. If they listen to him, well and good; if they don't listen to him, they will die, but Ezekiel will be exonerated; if Ezekiel fails to warn them and they die, their blood is laid at the prophet's door. After 587, when this office of watchman took effect, Ezekiel was no longer to preach the unconditional judgment of God, but he was to be God's helper in saving the people. Each individual in Israel was now his audience; he told them what it was necessary to do now. Some in his audience might have cynically claimed that their evil behavior was due to a propensity toward sin inherited from their fathers (18:2–20; cf. Ezek. 16, 20, 23). Yet no one could claim that his fate is fixed by his relative's behavior. (18:20). Others might have felt trapped in the behavior-pattern established in the earlier part of their own lives (18:21–32; 33:10–20). Individuals from both groups are urged by Ezekiel to turn and to live. Those who turn from their evil deeds will be granted the joys of God's presence. That is what seems to be meant by Ezekiel's offer of "life" (18:9, 17, 32). On the other hand, those who persist in doing evil will be denied access to God's presence; they will die (18:13).

The promised future in Ezekiel is solely the product of God's monergistic actions. Yet in the new age obedience will be expected, and even now, while the people still wait for the new day, they are urged to repent. Life is offered, but something more

is expected from the people than a lazy, complacent, lifeless wait-
ing for God to do it all. That "something more" is that even
now the people commit themselves to do God's will. Ezekiel's
role as watchman and his call for people to turn right now reflect
a creative tension found also in the message of Second Isaiah.
A faith clinging to the rays of God's dawning future must be a
faith active in obedience and love.

EZEKIEL'S MESSAGE OF HOPE

Because of the people's total corruption, Ezekiel neither announced nor desired any escape for Israel from Nebuchadnezzar's
sword. Yet his words after 587 abound with hope. Yahweh would
effect a new exodus followed by a return to Jerusalem, he would
be a good shepherd, and he would bring life to an Israel dead in
exile. This life could be described as an everlasting covenant,
marked by Israel's obedience and by abundant fertility in nature
and among the people. Israel would again have a prince like
David and would possess the land. Central to all Ezekiel's promises, however, was God's permanent dwelling with his people. To
express this promise, the prophet (or his followers) painted a
picture of the land arranged in symbolic zones of holiness radi-
ating from God's presence in the temple. A stream from that temple would bring about a new creation, including fertility to the
barren wastes of the Judean wilderness and life to the Dead Sea.
Ezekiel called his audience to repentance and assured them that
nothing—not even unfulfilled threats of invading enemies from
the north (cf. the defeat of Gog in Ezek. 38—39)—could ever disturb their security.

Ezekiel believed that God would be faithful to his old promises and that God was free to act beyond judgment and in creative ways. Part of God's creativity would manifest itself in provisions designed to protect future Israel from all dangers and
temptations. Part of his creative freedom was the way in which
he would make new Israel simply surpass the old. But the ultimate goal of all this faithfulness and freedom was to bring about
a universal "knowledge." Ezekiel anticipated a time when even
the nations would acknowledge and confess the one God: "Then
the nations will know that I am Yahweh."

CHAPTER 5

Yahweh Willing and Able

Second Isaiah's Response
to the Exile[1]

Sing, O heavens, for Yahweh has done it;
  shout, O depths of the earth;
break forth into singing, O mountains,
  O forest, and every tree in it!
For Yahweh has redeemed Jacob,
  and will be glorified in Israel.

(Isa. 44:23)

With such hymns of praise (cf. 42:10–13; 45:8; 49:13) the author of Isaiah 40—55 sang his message into the dark night of Israel's exile. Commonly known as Second Isaiah, his period of activity fell in the decade between 550 and 540. At a time when God's ability and willingness to save were seriously in doubt, Second Isaiah announced, "Israel will go home—in style!—to Jerusalem!" However joyful his message and however soaring his lyrical poetry, we dare not overlook the fact that Second Isaiah and his

1. I have been particularly helped by the following recent literature: Roy F. Melugin, *The Formation of Isaiah 40—55*, BZAW 141 (Berlin: Walter de Gruyter, 1976), a work which has broken much new ground in understanding the present arrangement of the book; C. R. North, *The Second Isaiah* (Oxford: Clarendon Press, 1964); Horst Dietrich Preuss, *Deuterojesaja: Eine Einführung in seine Botschaft* (Neukirchen-Vluyn: Neukirchener Verlag, 1976), good for up-to-date bibliography; Antoon Schoors, *I am God your Saviour*, VTSup 24 (Leiden: E. J. Brill, 1973), to my mind the best treatment of form-critical issues; Claus Westermann, *Isaiah 40—66*, OTL (Philadelphia: Westminster Press, 1969); and R. N. Whybray, *Isaiah 40—66*, NCB (Greenwood, S.C.: Attic Press, 1976).

message probably seemed unbelievable to his original audience. How he dealt with the doubts of his own people and the challenge presented by the ascendant Babylonian religion must occupy our attention in this chapter as much as the specific details of his good news about a new exodus, a new creation, and a new trip to Zion.

THE PROPHET'S CREDENTIALS

The book opens with an account of Second Isaiah's commission or call (40:1–8), that presents at once a summary of his central message and the reasons why that message should be believed. Like other prophets before him, Second Isaiah listened to the deliberations of the heavenly council (cf. Isa. 6; 1 Kings 22; Jer. 23:18). The first voice he heard admonished the angelic assembly to give comfort to God's people (vv. 1–2), here called "Jerusalem." "Comfort" in Second Isaiah can connote bringing Jerusalem's citizens home and rebuilding her ruins (52:9; cf. 49:13) or transforming her waste places into a virtual paradise (51:3; cf. 54:11). Israel's time of punishment, in any case, is declared over; she has already received double compensation for her sins (cf. Exod. 22:3, 6, 8).

A second voice (vv. 3–5) urged members of the heavenly council to construct a processional highway, flat and without curves, for Yahweh in the Arabian desert. When Yahweh would lead his flock on this highway from Babylon to Jerusalem, all peoples (all flesh) would see his glory.

The commissioning of Second Isaiah itself begins with the word *cry* shouted by a third voice (v. 6). Second Isaiah asks, "What shall I cry?" or perhaps better, "By whose authority shall I preach?" A voice from the council concedes that people and their fidelity are like grass or flowers that wither under God's hot wind from the desert. But one thing is sure, the voice continues, and it is the real source of Second Isaiah's authority and credibility: "The word of our God will stand for ever" (40:8; cf. v. 5).

The reliability of that word is demonstrated in the trial speeches against the nations or their gods, and Second Isaiah frequently invoked the authority of that word for his message by beginning a unit with the messenger formula, "Thus says Yahweh" (42:5; 43:1, etc.). In addition we read that Yahweh confirmed the prophet's message (44:26) and even put his own words into the prophet's mouth (51:16). God's coming victory over the nations is backed by an oath and a "word that shall not return" (45:23). What Yahweh speaks he always brings to pass (46:11). In the commission report and throughout this book of consolation, therefore, the word of God is set forth as a basis for confidence. Chaps. 40—55 end with a ringing reprise on God's word. Yahweh's reliability and effectiveness in dispatching rain and snow are matched by his word that always achieves its purpose in history (55:10–11). In this respect it differs totally from the fickle word of men (cf. 55:8–9). The credibility of the news about the new exodus and the credibility of the prophet himself rest on nothing less than God's abiding word. With such bold assertions the book begins and ends.

DIAGNOSING THE PROBLEM:
THE TRIAL SPEECHES AGAINST ISRAEL

Second Isaiah lacks the "reproaches" and "threats" that pervade preexilic prophecy, presumably since the punishment thereby threatened had already befallen Israel. In the three trial speeches against Israel contained in Second Isaiah, Yahweh responds to Israel's charge that he had arbitrarily abandoned it by raising counteraccusations against Israel.[2]

1. 42:18–25. Yahweh had been no heartless punisher, blind and deaf to Israel's suffering. Rather, he gave them up because they sinned against him and refused to obey his law. Israel itself is the one who is blind and deaf (cf. 42:16, 43:8).

2. 43:22–28. Yahweh had not burdened Israel with many cultic requirements, but they had loaded Yahweh down with their sins, iniquities, and rebellions. Their many sacrifices gave him no real honor. From the notorious sins of Jacob, their first father, to the rebellions of the priests and official prophets throughout their

---

2. For detailed discussions see Schoors, *I am God your Saviour*, pp. 189–207.

history, Israel had piled up a record that could lead to only one verdict—guilty—in a trial with Yahweh.

3. 50:1–3. Yahweh had not divorced Zion like a ruthless husband nor sold her citizens into slavery to pay his debts. Israel was sold because of her iniquities, mother Zion because of her rebellions. Yahweh's accusers do not dare show up for the trial (v. 2a). Does he lack power to redeem? Look at the record: He showed in Egypt and in the crossing of the Reed Sea what real power means (50:2–3).

The trial speeches against Israel are a major attempt by Second Isaiah to display God's willingness and ability to save. Israel's sin had led to abandonment and exile. Yet accusations of sin are followed by no new announcements of punishment in Second Isaiah. Instead, the prophet announced God's countervailing attitude:

> I, I am he
> who blots out your rebellions *for my own sake,*
> and I will not remember your sins.
>
> (43:25 RWK)

Yahweh's readiness to forgive comes from his own gracious initiative ("for my own sake"; cf. 42:21 and 48:11), and he displays thereby the kind of divine forgetfulness that is Israel's only hope. In another context Yahweh's forgiving nature is expressed in a moving simile drawn from nature: Israel's sinfulness will soon be put away as if it were clouds and mist (44:22). Yahweh has characteristics—namely, his compassion, his everlasting love, and his oath not to be angry—which contradict and overcome his decision to abandon Israel (54:7–10). His promises of grace are unalterable.[3]

The message of forgiveness contained in the trial speeches against Israel *and* in other portions of Second Isaiah shows that Yahweh is indeed willing to save. The prophet urged the exiles to prepare themselves through personal repentance to seek Yahweh and to call upon him (55:6–7; cf. 44:22). He desperately

3. See Bernhard W. Anderson, "Exodus and Covenant in Second Isaiah and Prophetic Tradition," *Magnalia Dei*, ed. F. M. Cross, W. E. Lemke, and P. D. Miller (Garden City, N.Y.: Doubleday & Co., 1976), pp. 338–60.

hoped for and pleaded for a return to the God "who will have mercy" and "abundantly pardon" (55:7).

IS YAHWEH ABLE? THE TRIAL SPEECHES AGAINST THE NATIONS OR THEIR GODS

Despite all the physical miseries that went along with the Exile, the most serious problem for the Israelites was theological. How could they believe in a God who lost the latest war? Why not worship the gods of Babylon whose armies, after all, were the winners? Second Isaiah deals with such questions in a series of trial speeches between Yahweh and the nations or their gods.[4] These speeches are defenses of Yahweh's claim to rule history and a radical denial of the counterclaim of the gods. Since the gods could not foretell the future, either in former times or in the current crisis, they are considered "nothings" (e.g. 41:24, 29).

In the trial speeches against the gods, Second Isaiah replaced the previously accepted proof for a god's divinity—his power to win military victory—with a different kind of proof: the dependable and unremitting continuity between what a real God *says* and what he *does*. This continuity between word and action is tested on the basis of Yahweh's and the gods' record in the "former things" and the "new things."

The term "former things" in Second Isaiah seems at times to be a specific reference to the power of God's word in effecting the Exodus from Egypt (43:16–18), but at other times it refers to Yahweh's past deeds in general, including, we believe, the fairly recent events of Jerusalem's destruction in 587.[5] The events of Israel's history in general seem to be meant when Yahweh says,

> The former things I declared of old,
> > they went forth from my mouth and I made them known;
> > then suddenly I did them and they came to pass.
> > > (48:3; cf. v. 5)

---

4. For discussion of both form and content, see Schoors, *I am God your Saviour*, pp. 207–45.

5. Cf. 41:22; 42:9; 46:9. See Odil Hannes Steck, "Deuterojesaja als theologischer Denker," *KD* 15 (1969): 280–93, especially p. 291, and Westermann, *Isaiah 40—66*, pp. 15–16.

That history included the catastrophic destruction of 587, which Yahweh had long threatened through the prophets. Hence the fall of Jerusalem, instead of being a sign of God's weakness, became an additional piece of evidence for his strength: it showed the truthfulness of Yahweh's prophets and of the word of God they proclaimed. Yahweh had said that exile was coming, and his own people were expert witnesses to the absolute fidelity of that word (43:9–10).

Since Yahweh's word had been proven reliable in the former things, Israel could—and should—trust it in the new things (42:9). New things can refer to the impending fall of Babylon and the rise of the Persian Cyrus (48:6 and 14; cf. 45:21; 46:11). Or new things can also mean the forthcoming new exodus and the festive procession through a luxuriant wilderness toward Jerusalem (43:19–20). After this introduction to the former and new things, we can now turn to a brief summary of the trial speeches themselves.

1. 41:1–5. The nations are here invited by Yahweh to witness his contest with the gods (v. 2) about who is in sovereign control of history. Since Yahweh alone stirred up the man of the hour, Cyrus, and gave him a series of breathtaking victories, the nations must tremble at this theophany (v. 5) and silently concede the correctness of Yahweh's claim. He rules history from beginning to end (v. 4).

2. 41:21–29. Yahweh challenges the gods in this speech to demonstrate their control of history by explaining the meaning of past events or predicting future ones. Exasperated at their silence, he exclaims, "Do good, or do harm, that we [= Yahweh and his council, or Yahweh and Israel] may be dismayed and terrified" (41:23b). In other words, "If you gods cannot explain the past or predict the future, at least do something so that we may know you gods have some kind of existence." Yahweh's own defense rests again with Cyrus, whose ascent he had been the first to predict to Zion/Jerusalem through Second Isaiah, a "herald of good tidings" (v. 27). The judgment on the gods: they, their works, and their images are nothing (vv. 24 and 29).

3. 43:8–13. By their silence the nations now concede that they have no proofs to bring that could substantiate the power of their

god. Israel, however, is Yahweh's witness (43:10, 12; cf. 44:8), who has experienced his gracious actions. Their witness in this case is not for the benefit of others but for themselves: "You are my witnesses, says Yahweh . . . that you may know and believe me and understand that I am he" (43:10). Though ostensibly directed against the pagan gods, the trial speeches are primarily intended to convince Israel of Yahweh's ability to save. In vv. 10–13 the monotheistic assertions are part of this apologetic.

4. 44:6–8. The gods are asked whether they can be considered like Yahweh.[6] If any think they are, they should bring proofs of their divine ability (v. 7). The categorical denial of the gods' existence in vv. 6–8 leaves no uncertainty about the outcome of this challenge.

In the present form of Second Isaiah this trial speech is followed by a satirical description of idol worship (44:9–20). Where do idols come from? They are trees cut down in the forest. With half of the tree's wood the idolator builds a fire to cook his food and warm his house; the other half he turns into an idol and prays to it: "Deliver me, for you are my god!" This satire turns the challenge of v. 7 into a taunt. How could fake deities ever predict the future?[7]

5. 45:18–25. Yahweh invites the survivors of the nations, that is, those nations who will be left after the coming defeat of Babylon, to tell who predicted the victory of Cyrus. Actually Yahweh's word foretold this turn of events long ago, and it is that same word that guarantees that the whole world will finally acknowledge Yahweh's universal and sole supremacy. Israel's coming triumph rests in the capable hands of Yahweh.

The pronounced monotheism in these trial speeches and throughout Isaiah 40—55[8] is crucial for the prophet's argument

---

6. Cf. 40:18, 25; and 46:5. See also the list of passages in C. J. Labuschagne, *The Incomparability of Yahweh in the Old Testament* (Leiden: E. J. Brill, 1966), p. 193.

7. Cf. 41:6–7 and 46:6–7. Many scholars hold vv. 9–20 to be secondary. We need to pay attention, however, to the function of such texts in their canonical context. See Melugin, *The Formation of Isaiah 40—55*, pp. 120–21.

8. See Hans Wildberger, "Der Monotheismus Deuterojesajas," *Beiträge zur Alttestamentlichen Theologie*, ed. H. Donner, R. Hanhart, and R. Smend (Göttingen: Vandenhoeck & Ruprecht, 1977), pp. 506–30.

about the credibility of Yahweh's word and of Israel's hope for the future; his monotheism is subservient to soteriological interests. Put differently, Second Isaiah fought the tendency to turn from Yahweh to the gods of victorious Babylon by offering a blistering critique of the captor's religion. Its gods are nothings, and its adherents must pass from the scene in embarrassed silence.

IS YAHWEH WILLING AND ABLE?
THE DISPUTATIONS IN SECOND ISAIAH

Immediately after the account of the prophet's commission (40:1-8) and the account of God's leading his flock home to Jerusalem (40:9-11), we find a series of disputations aimed at refuting mistaken notions about God which might hinder the joyful acceptance of his announced salvation.

1. 40:12-17. In these verses Yahweh is pictured as a giant for whom the creation of the world was mere child's play. He holds the world's waters in his palm and measures the sky by the breadth of his hand. Yahweh needs no helpers or counselors,[9] and compared with him all the nations are mere drops from a bucket or even absolute nothings. The prophet thus disputes Israel's feelings of discouragement by pointing on the one hand to God's size and his wisdom in creation, and to the puniness of all earthly enemies on the other.

2. 40:18-26. The prophet begins this disputation (or series of disputations) with a question: To whom will you liken God? Yahweh's incomparability is affirmed by a mocking speech against the idols (vv. 19-20) and by references to God's power in creation (vv. 21-22) and in history (vv. 23-24), where princes and rulers are easily uprooted by the blast of God's spirit (cf. 40:7). The prophet then repeats the question in dispute, but now as a direct citation of God: "To whom then will you compare *me*?" (v. 25). This time Yahweh's incomparability is demonstrated at the expense of the astral cult, which was of course quite prominent in Babylon (v. 26). Like the Priestly writer, however, Second Isaiah

---

9. Whybray has detected here a polemic against Babylonian religion. See *The Heavenly Counsellor in Isaiah xl 13-14* (London: Cambridge University Press, 1971).

held the stars to be fully under God's power. The Holy One created them and assigned them their proper—and limited—functions (cf. 45:12b). Compared with the nations, the gods, the princes and rulers, and even the central deities of the Babylonian astral religion, Yahweh is the only sovereign God. He has displayed his superiority and his power in creation and in his control of history. The initial disputations in this chapter, then, give a clear, affirmative answer to the question, Is Yahweh *able* to deliver Israel?

3. 40:27–31. With this final disputation of chap. 40, Second Isaiah touched on a different question: Is Yahweh *willing* to deliver? The prophet contested Israel's complaint that God disregarded their way and their right (v. 27) for the following four reasons: (a) Yahweh is an everlasting God, active in the distant past, the present, and the future; (b) as Creator of the ends of the earth his power knows no special limits; (c) a God who is completely sovereign over time and space can never be faint or weary; and most directly to the issue in question, (d) God's understanding is unsearchable, that is, he will act only when he thinks the time is ripe. On the basis of these affirmations Second Isaiah concluded that those who "wait on Yahweh" will renew their strength and like God himself never grow weary or faint (cf. 49:23).

In short, the disputations appeal to Yahweh's creative power and his dominion over history in order to leave no doubt that he *can* help his people and that he is in fact *willing* to do so. Nevertheless, his decision to deliver Israel via the pagan Cyrus (cf. 41:2–3, 25) evoked indignant reactions in Second Isaiah's audience.

CYRUS: GOD'S EFFECTIVE AND CONTROVERSIAL MESSIAH

We have no way of knowing how many accepted Second Isaiah's claim—which turned out to be correct!—that Cyrus would be the one to topple the Neo-Babylonian Empire. His clearest and most controversial word about him is a royal oracle of election (45:1–7) in which Yahweh designates the Persian king as his messiah, appoints him to defeat nations, kings, and cities (v. 1), and promises to prepare the way for his lightninglike triumphs (v. 2). Though Cyrus himself did not yet know the source of his victories (vv. 4–5), Yahweh promised to give him fabulous treasures which would lead him to recognize his elector (v. 3). The motivation for God's acting in this way is two-fold: (*a*) his commitment to his elect servant Jacob (v. 4), and (*b*) his desire that people everywhere confess that Yahweh is the only God (v. 6).

One can well imagine the consternation this oracle evoked within the exilic community. Why would God use a pagan to bring about his people's deliverance? Could there not be a new Moses, a new David, or even a new Josiah? Should the term *messiah*, which had long been associated with the occupants of the Davidic throne, be given to an avowed pagan like Cyrus? The prophet faced up to these questions in a series of disputations in which he both refuted those who felt Yahweh had no power and challenged those who were indignant over the choice of Cyrus.

1. 44:24–28. This disputation is permeated with hymnic elements. Vv. 24–26a, for example, give Yahweh's credentials in participial form: he is Israel's Redeemer and Creator; he frustrates oracle priests and the allegedly wise, but he confirms the word of his prophets. It is precisely this God, with these credentials, who says (*a*) to Jerusalem, "She shall be inhabited"; (*b*) to the cities of Judah, "They shall be built"; (*c*) to Cyrus, "My shepherd. He shall fulfill all my purpose"; and (*d*) to the temple, "Your foundations will be laid" (vv. 26–28). In the present arrangement of materials, this disputation is followed by the royal oracle of election addressed to Cyrus (45:1–7), a hymn (45:8), and a second disputation (45:9–13).

2. 45:9–13. According to this passage, Yahweh regards criticism of Cyrus as a direct challenge to his sovereignty, and he confronts his critics with sharp, accusatory questions: "Does a lump of clay ask the potter, 'What are you making?' Or does it offer the carping criticism, 'You forgot the handles on me, your pot?' Does a human ovum say to a potential father, 'What are you going to beget?' Or does a child cry out to his mother, 'What are you

giving birth to?' " Israel's audaciousness becomes apparent when Yahweh confesses that he is the Creator and that the choice of Cyrus is in accord with his nature and his plan of salvation. That Cyrus will be the one to build Jerusalem and set Yahweh's exiles free is good news and not bad. The clinching argument comes with an appeal to Yahweh's word itself: "Says Yahweh of Hosts" (v. 13; cf. 44:24).

3. 46:5–11. An initial question about the incomparability of Yahweh (v. 5) is followed by words mocking the idols whom some might consider rivals to Israel's God (vv. 6–7). A conclusion comes in v. 9: "I am God and there is no other . . . there is none like me." The prophet then added that God, who rules history with an irresistible plan, had also said:

> I call a bird of prey from the east,
>   the man of my plan from a distant country.
> I have surely spoken, and I will just as surely bring it to pass,
>   I have purposed, and I will just as surely do it.
>
> (v. 11 RWK)

God's word is invoked in this disputation to authenticate his right to raise Cyrus.

4. 48:12–15. This pericope first establishes the credentials of Yahweh (he created the world by his word; his prediction proofs establish his dominion over history) before it goes on to give a specific example of his rule:

> Yahweh loves him [= Cyrus];
>   and he shall perform his purpose on Babylon,
> and his arm shall be against the Chaldeans.
>
> (48:14; cf. v. 15 and 48:1–11)

From this survey of Second Isaiah's commission, his explication of God's word, the trial speeches, and the disputations emerges a picture of a most embattled prophet. Even good news is not easy to preach when one's audience doubts the ability or willingness of Yahweh to save, or when they refuse to accept salvation on God's terms. Salvation's source was God's free and unmerited forgiveness; its shape was the military successes of the pagan Cyrus. We must now spell out some details of this salvation.

GOD'S PROMISES: THE ORACLES OF SALVATION

Whereas accusations against Israel play a very minor role in Second Isaiah, promises to the exiles abound. Many of them appear in the oracles of salvation, perhaps the most emotional and tender type of speech employed in the entire prophetic corpus. These oracles are characterized by a spirit of joy, by intimate personal language, and by the assertion that there has already been a change from judgment to salvation. Some forty years ago, Joachim Begrich suggested that these oracles of salvation were modeled after a priest's response in the preexilic temple to individual psalms of supplication or laments.[10] This background would explain the many allusions in the oracles to typical complaints, and it would account for their warm language, since priests delivered their oracles personally to individuals in preexilic times (1 Sam. 1:17). Second Isaiah, according to the current version of this hypothesis, appropriated and imitated this form, which was intended originally for *individuals,* to speak words of assurance to the *whole people.* The characteristic features of these oracles will be demonstrated at the hand of 41:8–13.[11]

Address (41:8–9; cf. 41:14a, 44:1, 2b). These verses abound with references to election. Second Isaiah quite often connects Israel's election to her status as the servant of Yahweh (e.g. 42:1; 43:10), dependent on God's call and care. We should not miss the intimate and honored relationship suggested in biblical times by the term *servant.* The servant of the king, for example, was one of the top officials in the land, and the psalmist often bases his prayer precisely on his own servant status (e.g. 31:16; 35:27). The strong affirmations of Israel in the addresses anticipate the concrete good news which follows in the other parts of the oracles.

10. Joachim Begrich, "Das priesterliche Heilsorakel," *ZAW* 52 (1934) : 81–92. See also Schoors, *I am God your Saviour,* pp. 32–84; Melugin, *The Formation of Isaiah 40—55,* pp. 13–22; Westermann, *Isaiah 40—66,* pp. 11–13; and Thomas M. Raitt, *A Theology of Exile: Judgment/Deliverance in Jeremiah and Ezekiel* (Philadelphia: Fortress Press, 1977), pp. 151–58.
11. Three of the other five oracles of salvation have a section called "goal" (41:16b; 43:7; 44:5). God's actions for Israel, accordingly, have as their final goal the praise of Yahweh by Israel or by the nations.

Assurance of Salvation ("Fear not . . . be not dismayed," 41:10a; cf. 41:14a; 43:1b, 5a; 44:2b; 54:4a). This command had the power in itself to banish fear. Elsewhere we find such commands addressed (*a*) to people who were awestruck at a theophany of God (Gen. 15:1; Dan. 10:12); (*b*) to people whose fears of threats or dangers led them to bring a lament (Lam. 3:57); or (*c*) to Israelites when they were faced with threats from military enemies (Josh. 8:1). As exilic Israel heard these oracles of salvation, they, too may have been fearful because of Yahweh's presence in his word, anxious because of the threats and dangers of exile, and terrified because of the obvious superiority of Babylon's military might.

Nominal Substantiations[12] ("For I am with you . . . for I am your God," 41:10a; cf. 41:14b; 43:1b, 5a; 54:5). The assurance "I am with you" was all the equipment needed by a Moses (Exod. 3:12), a Gideon (Judg. 6:16), or a Jeremiah (1:8). Another nominal substantiation is "Your Redeemer is the Holy One of Israel" (41:14b). The term *g'l* is used of God some seventeen times in Second Isaiah, while there are only seven occurrences of this usage in all of our preexilic sources.[13] We can learn much about its theological meaning by examining its use in secular or legal contexts. (1) Israelites were to redeem a relative who had been compelled to sell himself into debt slavery (Lev. 25:47–55). (2) If a person was forced by poverty to sell his land, a kinsman had the first right to redeem (buy) it (Lev. 25:23–34; cf. Jer. 32:7–8; Ruth 4:4–6). (3) The "redeemer of blood" saw to it that the murder of his kinsman was avenged (cf. Num. 35:12, 19, 24, 25). (4) A blood relative was to marry the widow of a man who died without a male heir (Ruth 3:12–13). A redeemer in Israel, therefore, was one who acted as a kinsman on behalf of someone who was enslaved, injured, or in danger of losing honor or property.

Two oracles of salvation, 43:1–4 and 43:5–7, develop the kin-

12. These substantiations are called "nominal" since their verbs are only implicit in Hebrew.
13. For the statistics and a detailed discussion of this term see Carroll Stuhlmueller, *Creative Redemption in Deutero-Isaiah*, AnBib 43 (Rome: Biblical Institute Press, 1970), pp. 99–123.

ship aspects of the word *redeem*. Yahweh's kinship in these oracles is expressed in his assurance, "I have redeemed you" (v. 1), but it is also seen when he addresses Israel by its own name (v. 1) or when Israel is named after Yahweh (v. 7). Note also the reference to Israel as Yahweh's sons and daughters (v. 7) and the endearing words "You are mine" (v. 1) and "You are precious in my eyes, and honored, and I love you" (v. 4).

Yahweh promised his protecting presence for his kin on their way home from exile (43:2–3a), and he even offered to buy their release:

> I give Egypt as your ransom,
> Ethiopia and Seba in exchange for you.
> (43:3; cf. 4)

In other words, Yahweh promised to grant Cyrus temporal rule over all of then-known Africa in return for the freedom of enslaved Israel. What is more, he issued stern orders for the emancipation of his children from their captors (43:6; cf. 49:22ff.).

The kinship connotations of the word *redeem* help us to understand the equation of the term *redeemer* with the epithet "the Holy One of Israel" in the nominal substantiation cited above. The Holy One is transcendent, sovereign, or a God without compare (40:5), but he is also the Holy One *belonging to* Israel, the one who chose it (49:7b) and who will create its future (41:20).

The word *redeem* in Second Isaiah can refer to God's deliverance of Israel from Egypt or his leading them through the Reed Sea. Thus the prophet writes, "You made the depths of the sea a way for the redeemed to pass over" (51:10; cf. 48:20). Second Isaiah also links the term *redeem* to statements about Yahweh's power (54:5). Yahweh is not just to be a husband to his wife Zion, who feels abandoned by him and laments her lack of children; he is also her Maker-Creator. He is not just Israel's kinsman-redeemer, the God who chose her; he is at the same time the God of the whole earth. These assertions of power are underscored by the martial connotations of his name, Yahweh of hosts.

Verbal Substantiations ("I will strengthen you, I will help you, I will uphold you with my victorious right hand," 41:10; 41:14b, 43:1b, 54:6). What is not clear in this translation is that each of the verbs is in the perfect, or past, tense in Hebrew. That is, they could just as well be translated, "I have strengthened," "I have helped," and "I have upheld." These past tenses indicate that Yahweh has already turned to intervene on Israel's behalf. Once God's decision to save has been made, the deed is as good as done; the actual deliverance is totally predictable and even anticlimactic.

Outcome (41:11–12; cf. 41:15–16a; 43:2–4, 5b–6; 44:3–4; and 54:4b). The verbs in the outcome section are usually imperfect (= future), and they indicate in detail what will be the consequence of God's action. In 41:11–12, for example, we are told that the hostile nations surrounding Israel will vanish into thin air when Yahweh strengthens, helps, and upholds Israel. In another of the oracles, wormlike Israel is told she will become a threshing sledge to mow down the mountains and hills, thanks to Yahweh's help (41:15–16a).

THE NEW EXODUS

> Remember not the former things,[14]
>   nor consider the things of old.
> Behold, I am doing a new thing;
>   now it springs forth, do you not perceive it?
>   (43:18–19)

God's promised "new thing" refers to Israel's exodus from Babylonian exile, together with its causes and consequences. Second Isaiah urged Israel not to limit its theological horizons to

---

14. We must add a few words on the prophet's skillful use of the terms *remembering* and *forgetting*. Though Israel elsewhere was called to witness to God's past deeds, she is told in this verse to forget them. She lived in fear that God had forgotten her (49:14; cf. 40:27), but Yahweh assured her, I will never forget you (49:15; cf. 44:21). Israel's names graven on Yahweh's hands (49:16) and the permanently fertile desert (55:13) remind God of Israel (cf. the rainbow in P). In the future, Israel will no longer remember the shame of her widowhood when Yahweh separated himself from her (54:4). Yahweh himself will forget her sins (43:25).

a recounting of the old salvation history but to expect that God would be willing and able to bring off an exodus again as he had in the past. The first exodus, to be sure, had not lost all meaning. Israel's witness to Yahweh's earlier activity in fact was one basis for faith (43:9–10) in the Exile, and Yahweh's past direction of history was one basis for disputing the claims of the gods in the trial speeches. Nevertheless, God's impending act of salvation was his decisively new thing, hailed by a new song (42:10). This coming event was to run parallel to the old exodus, to escalate and heighten its themes, and even to supersede it.[15]

Israel would not go out in haste or in flight (52:12) as she did in the first exodus (Exod. 12:16; Deut. 16:3). Instead, Yahweh himself would march before and behind her in a manner similar to but presumably better than the pillar of cloud and fire of first wilderness days. No murmuring would mar the new trek through the wilderness. The mere announcement of the new exodus would evoke cascades of praise from the sea, its coastland, and the desert cities of Edom (42:11), and from the heavens, the depths of the earth, the mountains, and the forest (44:23; cf. 49:13). The captives were exhorted to lead the singing (48:20). All creation would echo Israel's own joy and give the exiles a mighty ovation (55:12).

THE WAY

Once free from Babylon, the Israelites would march home on a highway built by the angels across the Arabian desert (40:3). This "way" would be freed of all dips and hills and curves (40:4). Such a superhighway, of course, far outshines the trackless desert through which Israel's parents passed in Mosaic times. By heading straight across the desert it avoids the detour from Ur to Harran that had been taken, according to one tradition, by Abraham, and which was in fact the regular route from Babylon to Palestine. On this road Yahweh would advance on Jerusalem

15. See Anderson, "Exodus Typology in Second Isaiah," *Israel's Prophetic Heritage,* ed. B. W. Anderson and W. Harrelson (New York: Harper & Row, Publishers, 1962) , pp. 177–95.

like a warrior after military victories,[16] and he would be proclaimed as king (52:7; cf. 41:21; 43:15; 44:6).[17] Since kings were
customarily called shepherds in the ancient Near East, we should
probably see both pastoral and royal connotations in passages
which describe how Yahweh as shepherd would gather, lead,
water, and care for his flock (40:11 and 49:9–11; cf. Ezek. 34:
11–16). By providing food and water for the participants of the
new exodus (41:17–18; 43:19–20; 48:21; 49:10) Yahweh would
repeat the miracles of the first wilderness period, though with two
innovations: (*a*) He himself, not Moses or some other human
leader, would lead Israel through the desert and make water flow
from the rock (48:21). (*b*) His provision of food and water in the
desert would be a new creation. Yahweh would accordingly create
oases and pools in the desert and make all sorts of trees grow
there to give shade to the traveling Israelites (41:19). Instead of
thorn and briar, the desert would thrive with cypress and myrtle
(55:13). The scorching wind and the sun would lose their power
to harm Israel (49:10); aye, Zion's wilderness would become like
Eden, the garden of Yahweh (51:3). Even the wild beasts, the
jackals, and ostriches would honor Yahweh (43:20; cf. 11:6–9;
35:7; and Gen. 3:18).

A CULTIC PROCESSION TO A RENEWED ZION

The highway for the new exodus would be also a cultic way:

> Depart, depart, go out thence,
>   touch no unclean thing;
> go out from the midst of her, purify yourselves,
>   you who bear the vessels of Yahweh.
>   (52:11; cf. 35:8–9)

The vessels of Yahweh take the place of the ark of the covenant
used in preexilic processions, and of the vessels "borrowed" from

---

16. Yahweh is often pictured in military images in Second Isaiah; cf. 40:10;
42:13, 49:24–26; 51:9, 22–23; and 52:10. He was also the "man of war" at the
first exodus (Exod. 15:3, 6).
17. Ezekiel too affirmed Yahweh's kingship in the context of the new exodus
(20:33). Exod. 15 ends its account of the victory at the sea with the confession "Yahweh will reign forever and ever" (v. 18).

the Egyptians at the first exodus (Exod. 3:21–22; 11:2–3; 12:35–36). On this sacred highway a theophany of Yahweh would take place (cf. 40:5, 9).

The wilderness journey is to end with a procession to Zion. In 40:9 personified Zion and Jerusalem are urged to climb high mountains and announce to the cities of Judah Yahweh's victorious, theophanic march to Zion. The prophet even envisioned a messenger who would go ahead of the exile caravan to tell Zion of God's victory. The city's lookouts were to echo his cry as they witnessed the return of King Yahweh to Zion (52:7–8).

Zion is promised a rapid rebuilding[18] and repopulation. So massive will be the new population, in fact, that complaints of overcrowding will arise, leading Zion to marvel at how her barrenness in exile has been totally reversed (49:17–21; cf. 54:1–10). At least some of the population increase is to come from the large number of Zion's sons and daughters brought home by the nations. In the future all attacks on Zion will fail, since Yahweh created and therefore controls the blacksmith and the warrior. Even words cannot hurt Zion (54:11–17).

CREATION'S ROLE IN SECOND ISAIAH

Throughout Second Isaiah, also in the announcement of God's new actions, creation plays a major role; it undergirds, enriches, and expands. We have already seen how God's creation and preservation of the world provided the basis for affirming his ability and willingness to save (40:12–13). Affirmations about creation also supported God's credentials in his contest with the gods (45:18; cf. 40:25–26) and in his promise to free Israel from its tyrants (51:13–16). Since Yahweh laid the foundations of the earth and spread out the heavens, one could be certain that Cyrus would perform God's purposes on Babylon (48:13–14). Zion need not fear, since the soldier (the destroyer) and the weapons manufacturer (the smith) are creatures of Yahweh and therefore under his control (54:6).

---

18. The only mention of a new temple is in 44:28. According to 54:11–12, Jerusalem's new buildings will all be made of precious stones.

Creation language could be used to enrich Second Isaiah's idea of monotheism:

> I form light and create darkness,
> I make weal and create woe,
> I am Yahweh, who do all these things.
>   (45:7).[19]

That both good and evil are brought by Yahweh is a constant of Israelite religion (cf. Amos 3:6), but Second Isaiah achieved a breakthrough in extending this monergism back to creation itself.

Second Isaiah gave the events of Israel's salvation history a new dimension by describing them as creative acts. In several oracles of salvation, the credentials of Yahweh are in his "creation" of Israel, that is, in his acts of election and deliverance at the first exodus (43:1, 7; 44:2; cf. v. 21). The connection of creation and first exodus is also expressed in the images of 50:2 where God argues for his ability to save now by appealing to his cosmological/historical victories in the past. God's election of Israel and his care for them throughout their history are described elsewhere in metaphors of creation, birth, and preservation (46:3–4).

Yahweh, Zion's estranged husband who is willing to take her back, has confidence-inspiring credentials: he is her Creator (54:5). As Israel's Creator (45:9, 11), yes, as the Creator of the earth, man, the heavens, and the stars (45:12), Yahweh has the absolute freedom to direct history in the way he chooses (namely by using Cyrus). It is creation that provides reassurance that the meaning and relevance of the exodus traditions were not entirely lost in Israel's recent tragedies.[20]

Yahweh's past role as Creator is only a prologue to the future. He will bring life, water, and abundant trees to the barren desert and then be hailed as Creator once more (41:20). God's perform-

---

19. Coming at the end of an oracle announcing Cyrus' election, this verse may contain a subtle polemic against the dualism of his Persian religion. Second Isaiah elsewhere, however, seems unconcerned about polemicizing against *Persian* religion.

20. See Ph. H. Harner, "Creation Faith in Deutero-Isaiah," *VT* 17 (1967): 298–306.

ance at the first creation and the first exodus will be made almost
forgettable by the new creation he now undertakes, with its way
in the wilderness, rivers in the desert, and animals transformed
into agents of praise (43:16–21). Yahweh's creation is a "new"
thing (48:7).

Second Isaiah does not speak compartmentally of creation,
preservation, the election of Israel, Exodus, wilderness guidance,
new exodus, renewed wilderness, return to Zion. For him they are
all actions of Yahweh. In a celebrated hymn to the arm of Yahweh, it is not always possible to determine the point of transition
from one action to the next one (51:9–11). By using creation
terminology to describe all of God's actions, from the creation of
the universe to the new trip to Zion, Second Isaiah keeps a continuity in his theology. While the events he anticipates are new,
they are from the long-known Yahweh. There is not an old God
and a new one. Rather, Yahweh states, "I am the first and I am
the last" (41:4; 44:6; 48:12); "Yes, I am always the same" (41:4;
43:10, 13; 46:4; 48:12).

THE NATIONS

The foreign nations in Second Isaiah play an ambivalent and
paradoxical role. On the one hand, *Babylon's* imminent defeat
at the hands of Cyrus is a foregone conclusion. A taunt song in-
forms Dame Babylon that she will be humiliated and disgraced
like a prostitute (chap. 47). Though the song admits that Yahweh
was angry with Israel (v. 6), it castigates Babylon for showing the
captives no mercy, imposing heavy burdens on the aged, and not
considering the purpose of God's judgment (vv. 6–7). Babylon's
colossal arrogance and the skill of her astrologers will not be able
to avert the disaster and ruin that is coming her way (vv. 10–15;
cf. 46:1–2).

Second Isaiah also announced defeat for the *pagan nations in
general.* Israel's opponents would not only be shamed and con-
founded; they would also become as nothing at all (41:11–12).
Frail Israel herself (worm Jacob) would turn into a threshing
sledge to grind up her enemies (symbolized by the mountains and
hills), and the wind would blow their chaff away (41:15–16). The

agent of the nations' defeat is often Cyrus (41:25; cf. 41:2 and 45:1).

Another series of passages announce joyful deliverance from the tyrant's hand (51:12–16). Though Jerusalem is presently drunk from Yahweh's cup of wrath and her sons have fainted from this drink at every corner, Yahweh promises that the cup will soon be passed to those tormentors who have run roughshod over Israel's back. The cup of staggering will then be theirs alone (51:17–23)! The kings and queens who bring Zion's children home will become utterly subservient (49:23). In total defeat the oppressors will feed like cannibals on their own kith and kin (49:24–26). Once God had made David a witness to his divine power by granting him victory over many nations. Now, the promise made to David (the everlasting covenant) will be democratized, that is, it will be given to the whole people. At Israel's beck and call, the nations will come running to them as once they ran to David (55:3–5; cf. Ps. 18:43–44).

On the other hand, there are many passages which treat the nations much more positively. All flesh, for example, is to see Yahweh's theophany on the processional highway across the desert (40:5). The servant is twice described as a light to the nations (42:6 and 49:6). According to 49:6 (cf. 42:6), the servant's light enables the news of Yahweh's salvation victory to reach to the ends of the earth. Kings and princes of the nations will see and prostrate themselves (v. 7). What happens to the servant is a witness to the nations. Finally, Yahweh's commissioning and equipping of Cyrus is not just for the sake of his servant Jacob (45:4) nor only to enable Cyrus himself to recognize who it was who called him by name (45:5). Rather, here is the final reason for Yahweh's outfitting Cyrus:

> that men may know, from the rising of the sun
> and from the west, that there is none besides me;
> I am Yahweh, and there is no other.
>
> (45:6)

But does Second Isaiah think that these nations will come to believe in Yahweh? Does Israel have a "mission" to them? Or will the nations only be under Israel's rule? The principal evidence follows.

1. 44:1–5. In this oracle of salvation Israel is promised many offspring, but its population increase also seems to have an additional source:

> This one will say, "I belong to Yahweh,"
>   another will call himself by the name of Jacob,
> and another will write on his hand, "Yahweh's man,"
>   and surname himself by the name of Israel.
>
> (44:5 RWK)

Thus foreigners will see Israel's prosperity and seek to become part of Yahweh's people.

2. 45:14–17. Here too we are told of nations which will come over to Israel and be theirs. But these wealthy delegates come more as slaves than as proselytes (v. 14). Nevertheless, they acknowledge that God is with Israel alone, and they concede that other gods do not exist. All persistent idolators will be put to shame and confusion.

3. 45:18–25. In this trial speech, Yahweh announces that the gods cannot save the survivors of the nations, and he urges all the ends of the earth to be saved by turning to him. Yahweh's oath and word have set in motion a new course of history: "To me every knee shall bow, every tongue shall swear" (v. 23). Does the nations' oath in v. 23 represent only grudging acknowledgment of Yahweh's sole power, or is it the language of faith?

4. 53:4–5. The speakers in this fourth servant poem once despised the servant, but now they recognize that he had carried their griefs and sorrows. And more:

> He was wounded by our transgressions,
>   he was bruised by our iniquities;
> upon him was the chastisement that made us whole,
>   and with his stripes we are healed.
>
> (53:5 RWK)

This would seem to be the clearest evidence for a belief in "salvation" for the gentiles in Second Isaiah, but the interpretation of this and other servant poems is most uncertain.

Leaving aside for the moment this last passage, we can identify

the following motifs about the nations in Second Isaiah: (*a*)
Babylon and the other nations will be defeated; (*b*) the nations
will serve Israel by bringing home the exiles and by responding
as servants to her beck and call; (*c*) the nations will witness
Israel's future history and will be led to acknowledge the sole
power of Yahweh; (*d*) one passage seems to speak of proselytes
explicitly (44:5; cf. 55:5); (*e*) Israel is not sent on a mission to the
nations (they actually come to her), though her fate and posture
under God's governance may lead the nations to acknowledge
and confess Yahweh (cf. also the positive hopes for the nations
discussed in chaps. 3 and 4).

THE SERVANT OF YAHWEH

The servant poems (42:1–4; 49:1–6; 50:4–9; and 52:13—53:12)
are among the best-known and best-loved passages from Second
Isaiah, and they have been the object of an unprecedented
amount of scholarly research.[21] Yet it must be confessed that no
overall interpretation has achieved anything like a consensus.

Who is the servant? Two hypotheses dominate the discussion
today: (*a*) the servant is Second Isaiah himself and the poems are
autobiographical; (*b*) he is a personification of Israel. If the
poems are taken as autobiographical, many scholars suppose that
the prophet was either executed (so Preuss) or that he was imprisoned for a time by the Babylonians (so Whybray). Second
Isaiah indeed was a most embattled man, but evidence that he
experienced foul play comes only from the servant poems themselves, and even that evidence is vague and ambiguous. Since the
term *servant* (singular) in texts outside the servant poems themselves always refers to Israel, it is hard to believe it had a different meaning within the poems. What is more, the servant is
explicitly identified with Israel in the second poem (49:3; cf.
49:7), and the vocabulary used to describe the servant's election
(42:1) denotes the election of Israel elsewhere.[22] Those who fol-

---

21. For recent bibliography see Preuss, *Deuterojesaja*, pp. 117–18, nos. 122–
28a.

22. Jorg Jeremias, "*mišpāṭ* im ersten Gottesknechtlied (Jes xlii:1–4)," *VT* 22
(1972) : 40.

low the autobiographical hypothesis, especially if they believe the servant died, must ascribe the fourth poem to the prophet's disciples.

To identify the servant with Israel, however, is also not without serious problems. Not only must one propose an intense personification, which gives the picture of the servant its highly individualistic traits, but the second poem assigns the servant a mission *to* Israel (49:6), just after it has identified him *with* Israel. Melugin has suggested that the reason for this ambivalence stems from the fact that Second Isaiah himself was Israel in a very real sense. His task was Israel's task; his word was the word of Israel the servant. His ministry was a kind of archetype for the mission of Israel. Second Isaiah cannot be separated from Israel. Rather, he loses his personal identity in the chosen people.[23] In the interpretation which follows, I shall follow a middle position. The servant will be seen as Israel, but I concede that certain aspects of the servant's description have been shaped by reflections on the career of Second Isaiah.

1. 42:1–4. In these verses Yahweh announces to an unidentified audience his servant's election, the gifts with which he has been endowed, and the task for which he has been selected. Three times we are told that the servant will be responsible for "justice." What this means can only be understood in the light of the larger context.[24]

According to 40:14, Yahweh is the only source of that *mišpāṭ* which shapes the course of history, but this assertion is followed by Israel's complaint that her own *mišpāṭ* is disregarded by God (40:27). If God would only regard Israel's claim on his attention, they assert, history would change drastically: the pagan nations would no longer be in control.

Chap. 41 can be seen as one response to Israel's complaint. At the conclusion of the trial speech against the gods, the nations are said to tremble because they recognize that Israel's God is in control of history (v. 5). In the following oracles of salvation, on

23. Melugin, *The Formation of Isaiah 40—55*, pp. 146–47, 154–55, 169.
24. See W. A. Beuken, "*mišpāṭ*: The First Servant Song and its Context," *VT* 22 (1972) : 1–30, which I summarize and adapt in the discussion below.

the other hand, Israel is urged not to fear (vv. 10, 14), for her enemies will perish (vv. 11–12), and she will mow down all the obstacles, including the nations and their rulers, who keep her from returning home. Vv. 17–20 assert the validity of Yahweh's rule, and they are followed by another trial speech (vv. 21–29) in which the gods of the nations are categorized as "delusion" and "nothing." Not only does this conclusion contradict the complaint 40:27, but it also highlights the good news at the beginning of the following servant poem. Compare "Behold, they [the gods] are a delusion" (41:29) with "Behold, my servant whom I uphold" (42:1).

The first servant poem itself offers an interpretation of how God's justice over the nations will be carried into effect. Though the servant is the agent of Yahweh to establish his justice in history, he will not be raucous (v. 2; cf. 53:7) or ruthless (v. 3a). Wherever he meets weakness, whether in the nations or in Israel, he will not strike the final blow against those who are bruised and fainting. This concern for the weak reappears in the third (50:4) and fourth (53:4) poems.

At the end of 42:3 we are told that the servant will bring forth justice "to faithfulness," that is, until Yahweh's faithfulness is apparent. Finally, Yahweh announces that the servant will establish *mišpāṭ* in the earth, that is, he will proclaim the statute appropriate to the new situation brought about by God's just rule, and the coastlands wait eagerly for this law (v. 4). The words "He will not fail or be discouraged till" (42:4) hint that hard times are coming for the servant. Each of the following poems relates how the servant does not perish under the oppression he experiences while completing his task (49:4; 50:6; 53).

2. 49:1–6. The personified servant reports his own commission in this second poem. After calling the nations to attention (v. 1a), he reports how Yahweh called him before his birth and made his mouth like a sharp sword (vv. 1b–2). Jeremiah too was called prenatally and given a well-equipped mouth (1:4–9). Perhaps servant-Israel is to be understood as the embodiment of the prophetic office, just as the promises to King David have been transferred to all the people (55:3).

Designated as God's servant (v. 3) the speaker complains about the futility of his task (v. 4a) but follows this with an expression of confidence: "Surely my right is with Yahweh" (v. 4b). This assertion contradicts and corrects Israel's earlier complaint: "My right is disregarded by my God" (40:27). Vv. 5–6 offer God's plan for the servant. It is not enough for him to bring back Jacob-Israel; he is also to be a light to the nations. Thus the servant discovers that complaints about one's vocation only lead to a greater assignment (cf. Jer. 12:5–6). Israel will be a light to the nations, according to the present context, when her tribes are raised up (v. 6) and she is restored to the land (v. 8). Then the kings and rulers will see that the deeply despised, abhorred Israel, the doormat of the world powers, is really the property of faithful Yahweh, the elect people of the Holy One of Israel (v. 7).

3. 50:4–9. In this poem the servant commits himself to his vocation even in the face of opposition. Like the servant of the first poem (42:3), and like Yahweh himself (40:29–31), the servant helps and sustains those who are weary (v. 4). He is not rebellious (cf. Jer. 1:6–7; Ezek. 2:8) but voluntarily accepts physical abuse (v. 6) and expresses his absolute confidence that Yahweh will finally help him. In fact, he resolutely challenges his opponents (cf. Jer. 1:17–18; Ezek. 3:8–9), since he knows that Yahweh is the final and only arbiter of his case (vv. 7–9; cf. 49:4). Whether the servant here is Second Isaiah or the ideal Israel, his open ear contrasts with the deafness of empirical Israel (48:8). The verses that immediately follow the servant poem continue the description of fidelity under pressure. Yahweh's servant trusts in God even when he walks in darkness. That was Israel's vocation in the uncertain days of exile. Meanwhile, the unfaithful opponents of the servant show no such trust. They kindle torches and are sentenced to lie down in torment (vv. 10–11).

4. 52:13—53:12. Yahweh begins the first unit by foretelling the ultimate victory of his servant Israel (52:13–15). Though often a disgusting figure to the many (= the nations, cf. vv. 14–15), the servant's coming preeminence will "startle" these nations and make their kings shut their mouths in amazement.

Chap. 53 itself opens with a confession by these same nations and their kings. In their eyes the servant had been a figure despised by both God and men (vv. 2b–3, 4b), but suddenly they came to a different opinion (v. 4a). The sufferings of this stricken and afflicted servant came from bearing the sicknesses and pains of the nations, from his suffering in their stead and for their sins (53:5–6).

Led away (into exile? cf. 52:5) after imprisonment and trial, the servant was beaten for his people's rebellion (v. 8) and condemned to death and dishonorable burial, even though he had not committed violence or practiced deceit (v. 9).

At the poem's end[25] Yahweh promises the servant a reward for his faithfulness. No longer weak and crushed, the servant takes his place among the great ones of the earth because he risked his life to the uttermost and was classified with the rebels. As sin bearer (53:12b) the servant might be compared with the goat designated for Azazel on the Day of Atonement (Lev. 16:22) or even with the prophet Ezekiel who lay on his side to bear the sins of Israel (Ezek. 4:4–8). By praying for sinners (53:12b) the servant continues a long tradition in Israel of the righteous interceding for others who are sinful.[26]

We can summarize briefly our interpretation of the servant who is Israel. He will be the agent of God's rule of history, but this means neither a total annihilation of the nations nor a trouble-free life for the servant himself (42:1–4). In addition to his concern for the weak and weary within Israel, he must also

---

25. Vv. 10–11 cannot be translated with any certainty. They seem to indicate that the servant's suffering results from Yahweh's good pleasure and that the servant offers his life as a guilt offering (Lev. 5:14ff.). Long life is granted him, perhaps a reference to dead Israel's "resurrection" from the Babylonian exile. Cf. Ezek. 37:1–14.

26. Cf. Abraham (Gen. 18:22–32); Moses (Exod. 32:11–14, 32); Amos (7:1–6); Jeremiah (7:16; 11:14; 15:1), and Ezekiel (14:14–20). David J. A. Clines, *I, He, We and They: A Literary Approach to Isaiah 53*, *JSOT* Supplementary Series 1 (Sheffield, 1976), offers a structuralist or "language-event" interpretation of this passage. For him the figure of the servant "seizes" the readers and bends them to a new understanding of themselves and the direction of their lives (p. 63). Clines makes no attempt to integrate this reading into the message of Second Isaiah as a whole, but the poem, read in the structuralist mode, would not have had an *essentially* different message for people who had heard the news of a coming deliverance from Second Isaiah than that which I have outlined above.

be a light to the nations (49:1–6). Despite his troubles, the servant will maintain steadfast trust, knowing that Yahweh will finally vindicate him (50:4–9). The nations will be amazed when they see how God glorified him, while the servant learns the deeper meaning of his sufferings. Via them he carries the punishment intended for the nations, and it is for these nations he prays (52:13—53:12).

A CONCLUDING WORD

Second Isaiah lived late in the Exile. His audience was afflicted with doubts about God's willingness and his ability to save, and with questions about who was really in control of history. To them the prophet announced a great new exodus and a trip home to Zion, an announcement undergirded and enriched with references to Yahweh as Creator and Redeemer. By trial speeches, disputations, and appeals to God's word, Second Isaiah showed that Yahweh was able and willing to save.

This good and joyful news was promised by God in accord with his freedom. That freedom permitted him to use Cyrus as his special agent and to offer the oppressive nations both defeat *and* an opportunity to recognize whose was the real glory in the world. All this was grounded, at the beginning and end, and through the entire sixteen chapters of this book, in the word or promise of God proclaimed to weak and weary Israel.

As Israel waited for this word to happen, she was called to conduct herself as God's servant. Exile was seen, therefore, not just as a penalty to be paid by Israel or a condition from which she was to be delivered. Rather, Israel's faithful endurance of exile and her victorious emergence from it were designed to make her a light to the nations.

CHAPTER 6

When Memory Is Hope

The Response to Exile in P¹

The Priestly writing in the Pentateuch wrestles with the problems of exile through its retelling of the primeval history and of Israel's history before the conquest. This focus on the past is no mere literary technique; rather, P proposes that God will be present with his people, thereby actualizing his ancient promises to Noah and the patriarchs, precisely under the conditions mediated by Moses to the cultic community during the wilderness wanderings.

---

1. It is here assumed that the materials of P were once part of an independent source, not merely editorial additions made in the course of the Pentateuch's redaction. See Norbert Lohfink, S.J., "Die Priesterschrift und die Geschichte," *Congress Volume: Göttingen, 1977*, VTSup 29 (Leiden: E. J. Brill, 1978), pp. 189–225. Per contra Frank Moore Cross, *Canaanite Myth and Hebrew Epic* (Cambridge, Mass.: Harvard University Press, 1973), pp. 293–325. We follow Lohfink and others in distinguishing between a basic priestly document (Pᴳ) and various later expansions which incorporated additional, primarily legal material (Pˢ). For an authoritative list of passages in Pᴳ see Karl Elliger, "Sinn und Ursprung der priesterlichen Geschichtserzählung," *ZTK* 49 (1952): 121–22. In this chapter the terms P and Priestly writer refer primarily to the materials of Pᴳ. P ended either with the death of Moses (Martin Noth, Cross) or with a few additional passages found in Joshua (Lohfink, and Joseph Blenkinsopp, "The Structure of P," *CBQ* 38 [1976]: 275–92). P probably was written in Babylon during the Exile (Cross and Lohfink). The author gave his work a clear structure by his use of the ten Toledoth formulas ("These are the generations of...") and by travel notices drawn from an old desert itinerary (Cross and Lohfink). Lohfink has called attention to a series of paired events scattered throughout P that help us see which things the writer considered important. Cf. also Blenkinsopp.

CREATION AND SABBATH

While the sixth day and its works of creation represent a very high moment in P, it is the seventh day toward which his whole creation account flows. The seventh day was the first day set aside as "holy"; it also received a blessing (Gen. 2:3), just as the animals (1:22) and men and women did (1:28). We read of God's joyful satisfaction on the Sabbath with what had been completed in creation, a satisfaction which men and women, presumably, are supposed to share.

Observing the Sabbath in Babylon, whatever had been its history in earlier Israel,[2] would have been a highly confessional act, making Israel stand out sharply from its environment—Sabbath was not observed by Israel's Babylonian conquerors. Many of the exiles would have been tempted to ignore the Sabbath observance lest they make unnecessary waves. Such lack of observance, given the historical context, would mean a fateful step back from identifying oneself with God's chosen community. The Priestly creation story counters such backsliding by noting that Sabbath keeping fits into the God-given structures of the world. It is so important that even God himself kept a Sabbath as a climax to the very first week of the world's existence. One could easily draw conclusions from the greater to the lesser: if Sabbath is kept by God, how much more should it be kept by faithful Israelites.[3]

The emphasis on Sabbath in P's creation story is part of an attempt to preserve Israel's identity by linking the Sabbath to creation and by grounding its observance in an imitation of God himself. Sabbath keeping indicates whether one stands within Israel or not. As we shall see below, the other great mark of

---

2. For the latest survey of the Sabbath, its history, and theology in Israel, see Niels-Erik A. Andreasen, "Recent Studies of the Old Testament Sabbath," *ZAW* 86 (1974) : 453–69.

3. Cf. also Exod. 16:22–27; 20:8–11, where obedience to the Sabbath command is related to creation; Exod. 31:12–17, where Sabbath keeping is called an everlasting covenant and a sign between Yahweh and Israel; and Exod. 35:1–3.

Israelite religious identity, circumcision, is also given high status in P.

CREATION AND P'S ANTHROPOLOGY

In P's discussion of the image of God we find a second significant contribution to exilic theology in his creation account (Gen. 1:26–28; 5:1; 9:6). The events of the first six days proceed with a measured but irresistible cadence until 1:26, but then God took counsel with himself before completing the peak of his creation pyramid. God created man and woman simultaneously and as equals in his sight; he made them both in his own image. Exactly what is meant by this "image" has long been discussed. Are men and women a kind of statue set up by God to indicate his control of the world even in his absence? Does the image consist in being able to respond to God's will, a talent presumably possessed only by the human family? Or are people placed in the world with the primary role of being rulers, vice-presidents in charge of God's estate? Perhaps each of these interpretations has some claim to legitimacy, but the rulership designation seems to be the primary intention. In Gen. 9:6 we are told that the image of God continues in force after the flood, though with modification: animals can now be killed for food without that counting as violence (Gen. 9:2–3; cf. 1:29–30). The killing of humans, however, is totally prohibited: "For God made man in his own image" (9:5–6).

P tells his exilic audience that they are not really or merely prisoners of war, homesick and angry deportees, or the remnants of a once-proud aristocracy. Rather, they really are the kings and queens of God's estate, his agents in charge of the world. In P's own phraseology: they are—even after their disaster—men and women created in the image of God.

But P's radical anthropology can only be fully appreciated when it is compared with that of Babylonian theology and its view of creation and man as presented in Enuma elish (*ANET* 60–72). After Marduk, the god of Babylon, had killed the rebel goddess Ti'āmat in single combat and consigned her hapless consort Kingu to the charge of the god of death, he sliced Ti'āmat like a shellfish in two parts, forming the sky from the upper part of her body and, presumably, the earth from the lower half. Later Marduk responded to the gods' complaints about their heavy work by proposing that mankind be created from the blood of Kingu, the ringleader of the erstwhile revolt. On the people created by Marduk would be imposed the heavy work formerly done by the gods. Accordingly, human beings have two major defects: (1) their vocation is to do the dirty work of which the gods grew weary, that is, man's toil lets the gods be free; and (2) human beings are *essentially* evil since they are created from the blood of the chief rebellious deity.

Viewed against this backdrop, the role of human beings in the Priestly work takes on sharper contours. Perhaps one can even detect a polemic directed against the ideology of the Babylonian realm. Human beings are servants in the biblical perspective too, but theirs is a kingly, royal service that brings with it much status. Furthermore, far from being essentially evil, men and women—like the rest of creation—are called "very good" (1:31).

The polemic against the Babylonian religion in Genesis 1 may also be seen in the complete lack of dualistic or polytheistic conflict. No trace of a figure like Ti'āmat can be found, unless it be in the word "deep" (Gen. 1:2), which is probably related only etymologically to the Babylonian word Ti'āmat. While the Babylonians spoke of the dangerous monsters of sky, land, and sea, Genesis 1 mentions only that all fowl and the land and sea animals were created by God on the fifth day of creation. In Babylonian religion the sun and moon gods, Shamash and Sin, were prominent and popular deities, but the biblical writer has reduced the function of these luminaries to that of a clock, or a calendar, or a lamp giving light to the earth (v. 14). The stars, whose movements were searched by ancient astrologers for guidance and the like, show up almost as an afterthought in v. 16. The sun and the moon are not even given the identity and respect inherent in a name. They are but the "big one" that rules the day and the "little one" that rules the night.

CREATION AND THE WORD OF GOD

Vv. 3–5 of Genesis 1 illustrate a tightly composed pattern, which recurs throughout the chapter (vv. 6–8, 9–10, 11–13, 14–19, 20–23, 24–31): declarative formula ("And God said"); command ("Let there be light"); execution ("And there was light"); approbation ("And God saw that the light was good"). God's word of command that brings about creation is the same word which causes the later events in history. If anything special happens in history, a word of God must previously have gone forth—such is the priestly view.[4] The flood is called forth by God's speech to Noah (Gen. 6:13–21), and events like the covenant with Abraham (Gen. 17), the mission of Moses (Exod. 6), the plagues in Egypt (Exod. 7ff.), the crossing of the Reed Sea (Exod. 14), or the erection of the tabernacle (Exod. 25ff.) happen because Yahweh has given a command which must be carried out.

Many of these commands are followed by notices about specific human beings who carried God's wishes out (Noah, Gen. 6:22; Moses and Aaron, Exod. 7:6; cf. 39:32, 42–43; 40:16). Westermann observes that such human agents are naturally impossible in the creation account, but that, nevertheless, the Priestly writer maintains the unbreakable sequence of God's command and its actualization. Just as the command to Noah is the real event which releases the flood, so the command at creation is sufficient to create light, the firmament, or whatever, regardless of the presence or absence of a human agent. The idea that God's word will always be carried out even without a human agent applies also, in our view, to God's words of promise after creation, such as "I will be God for you and your descendants" (Gen. 17:7). In such cases human agents are not so much impossible as they are inappropriate.

In exile, when God's promise to Noah or Abraham might seem

---

4. Claus Westermann, *Creation* (Philadelphia: Fortress Press, 1974), p. 42; and idem, *Genesis*, BKAT 1/1 (Neukirchen-Vluyn: Neukirchener Verlag, 1974), p. 555. See also A. Eitz, *Studien zum Verhältnis von Priesterschrift und Deuterojesaja* (Heidelberg Dissertation, 1970), p. 90.

to be nothing but "words, words, words," P could remind his readers that the words, commands, or promises of God are no vacuous thing. By words of command God made the world. Back then at creation, or now in the crisis of exile, he needed no human helpers for his word to be effective.

CREATION AND FERTILITY

The command/promise for humans to be fruitful and multiply repeats itself time and again in the Priestly work. In Gen. 1:28 it is added to the statement about men and women being created in the image of God: "And God blessed them, and God said to them, 'Be fruitful and multiply and fill the earth.' "[5] This command/promise has its first fulfillment in the ten-generation Toledoth of Genesis 5.

The promise reappears in Gen. 9:1. This promise to Noah, the father of all postdiluvian humanity, also works: the Toledoth in Genesis 10 (the table of nations) lists the numerous offspring of Noah's three sons. Since these offspring are (the fathers of) all the nations of the world, Genesis 10 is a particularly powerful attestation of the power inherent in the fertility promise. The Toledoth genealogy of Shem in Gen. 11:10–26 adds further evidence for the efficaciousness of this blessing.

With Genesis 17, however, we find a major shift in emphasis. Here the fertility promise given to man and woman at creation and to Noah after the flood is extended—or limited—to Abraham the father of the people Israel, and it is linked directly to an everlasting covenant (vv. 2–6). By the double use of the adverb "exceedingly" (*mĕ'ōd*) in vv. 2 and 6, P indicates the sureness of the promise and the fullness of the expectations therein contained. He etymologizes the patriarch's new name Abraham as "father of a multitude of nations," thus giving added stress to the

---

5. Walter Brueggemann has detected in the commands to be fruitful and multiply the kerygma of P and has interpreted the whole fertility blessing as referring primarily to the gift of the land. See "The Kerygma of the Priestly Writers," *ZAW* 84 (1972): 397–414, reprinted in *The Vitality of Old Testament Traditions* (Atlanta: John Knox Press, 1975), pp. 101–13.

fertility promise. Abraham's great fruitfulness is to result in his siring nations (Israelites, Ishmaelites, and Edomites; cf. Gen. 12:3 J) and kings (that is, the Israelite monarchy). The promise's unilateral character is underscored by the great ages (100 and 90) of Abraham and Sarah.

But it is Jacob who is the real "man of blessing" in P's view.[6] In the central text (Gen. 35; cf. 28:3 and 48:4) God appears to Jacob at Bethel after his return from Paddan-Aram, blesses him, and says: "I am El Shaddai: be fruitful and multiply; a nation and a company of nations shall come forth from you, and kings shall spring from you" (v. 11 RWK). The changing of Jacob's name to Israel (v. 10) foretells his destiny: his descendants will become the people Israel. By adding a list of Jacob's sons born in Paddan-Aram (35:22b–26) the Priestly writer demonstrated how the fertility promise became a reality within the patriarch's own lifetime. In Exod. 1:1ff. P presents a similar list, but under the rubric "the sons of *Israel* who went to Egypt with Jacob." From Exodus 1 on, the nation Israel assumes center stage in P's account. Jacob, the man of blessing, has brought forth the nation with whom the covenant made with Abraham would be concretized and actualized.

Two additional notices in P bring the fertility theme and the Jacob story to a climax: "And [Israel] gained possessions in it [Egypt], and were fruitful and multiplied exceedingly (Gen. 47:27b); "But the descendants of Israel were fruitful and swarmed; they multiplied and grew strong exceedingly exceedingly; so that the land was filled with them" (Exod. 1:7 RWK).

The promises of fertility in Genesis 1, 9, 17 and 35 have been fulfilled repeatedly and, last of all, in—of all places!—Egypt, a land where Israel had lived in a kind of exile. The Priestly writer seems to be promising to his audience that they too might expect the fulfillment of the fertility promise made to *all people* at the creation and after the flood, and to *Israel* in the accounts of

---

6. Walter Gross, "Jakob, der Mann des Segens," *Bib* 49 (1968): 321–44, has developed a contrast between Abraham, the man of covenant, and Jacob, the man of blessing.

Abraham and Jacob. The exilic community could expect a fulfillment since the fertility promise was part of the everlasting commitment, or covenant, to Abraham.

THE FLOOD

When we turn to P's account of the flood, we come upon three additional ways in which the writer responded to exile. We refer to his understanding of sin, of an everlasting covenant, and of God's remembering. In each case we will describe the motif as it occurs in the flood account and as it appears in later sections of P.

SIN IN THE PRIESTLY WRITER[7]

It is most striking that P has no account of the Fall, Cain and Abel, the sin of Canaan, or the golden calf. Even when P repeats stories from the epic sources which reported mankind's sins, he often changes them radically by removing the specific mention of sin.[8] These omissions or reinterpretations lend greater importance to those few passages where P does report the sins of mankind in general, the sins of the political leaders and the people, and the sins of Moses and Aaron, the mediators of Yahweh. Lohfink has called the sins mentioned in these accounts *Ursünden* (primeval or original sins). P's intention is not so much to write history as to show the beginning of and a primitive picture of everything which will happen later. These sins foreshadow the sins which are rampant in P's own audience.

The sin of mankind in general is designated as "violence" in P's flood story (Gen. 6:11 and 13). Violence is the injustice people do to one another, their irresponsible oppression and inconsiderate violation of one another. As such it is a challenge to God, and it corrupts the good creation (6:11–12). Over against

7. The following section is largely a summary and retracing of the work of Lohfink, "Die Ursünden in der priesterlichen Geschichtserzählung," *Die Zeit Jesu,* ed. G. Bornkamm and K. Rahner (Freiburg: Herder, 1970), pp. 38–57.
8. The scattering of the people in Gen. 10:32 is a blessing in P, not the result of the sin of the Tower of Babel as it was in J. Jacob did not flee because he had cheated his brother out of the blessing but because he ought not to marry a local Hittite as his brother Esau had done (28:1–2, 7; cf. 26:34–35; 27:46).

such a picture the Priestly work holds up Noah as a righteous man, perfect in his generation. He walked with God (6:9) as had Enoch (cf. 5:22, 24). When Abraham was commanded to walk before God and be perfect (17:1), he was really being urged to live like Noah and so to avoid the violence that is common to all mankind. Exilic Israel knew from her prophets that she too had done such violence.[9] Her potential sin, according to P, was one she had committed in the past, and it is the common failing of all mankind: violence.

But there was also a sin—an original sin—done by Israel's political leaders and the entire people in the desert. They slandered or despised the saving gift of the land (Num. 13:32; 14: 36–37). Because of the spies' evil report (13:32) the people murmured (14:2), rejecting the gift of the land and even the Exodus itself (14:3); they became an evil congregation (14:27). Lohfink has proposed that the leaders of the exilic community, and the masses whom they misled, did not listen to God's exhortation to return to the land and no longer wanted to have this land and live in it since they no longer thought highly of it (cf. Ezek. 36). Just as the original spies led the rest of the people to sin (Num. 14:2 and 36), so the political leaders in exile faced a similar temptation to mislead the people. In wilderness times the people expressed their disdain for the land by wishing they had died in Egypt or that death would overtake them now in the wilderness (14:2). This last request was literally fulfilled (14:28–29 and 35), and its message for exilic Israel would be unmistakable: despising the saving gift of the land can only lead to death outside the land for the sinful generation.

As a contrast to these rebels the Priestly work holds up Joshua and Caleb as models. They considered slander against the land blasphemy against the God who gave it, and so they rent their clothes (14:6). Through their good report of the land (14:7) they avoided the sin of the other leaders and of the masses. Because they displayed the proper relationship to God, they were the only ones in their generation who were allowed to enter the land.

9. Cf. Amos 3:10; Mic. 6:12; Jer. 22:3; Ezek. 7:23 and 12:19.

The third original sin involved the spiritual or religious leaders. This is the sin of Moses and Aaron, who sinned when they brought water from the rock at Kadesh (Num. 20:1–13). Moses' words, "Shall we bring forth water for you from the rock?" displayed the uncertainty of a question instead of the confidence of a command (20:10). The exilic religious leaders, according to this understanding of P, were in danger of failing to trust in and proclaim the miraculous power of Yahweh, which is capable of doing the impossible (cf. v. 12).

EVERLASTING COVENANTS IN THE PRIESTLY WRITER

As a conclusion to the flood account, P presents God's covenant with Noah, the first of his everlasting covenants (Gen. 9:8–17). The covenant's unilateral, promissory character is brought out in a number of ways. It is called "my" (= God's) covenant (vv. 9, 12, 15); it is never called Noah's. While the technical term for making a covenant in the epic sources is to "cut a covenant," a term which perhaps denoted the performance of symbolic sanctions against potential violators of the covenant at a cultic ceremony, the covenant with Noah is not cut, it is "given" (v. 12; cf. 17:2) or "established" (v 17; cf. 17:7 and Exod. 6:4). This covenant is decreed, given by God's orders. The promissory character is also denoted by the sign of the covenant, the rainbow, intended to refresh God's memory.

This unilateral covenant will last forever. It will be valid for Noah and his sons, their descendants, and all the creatures who came from the ark (vv. 9–10) for perpetual generations (v. 12). The term *everlasting* was used by Ezekiel to indicate the unbreakable character of the *new* covenant of peace which God plans for the exiles (Ezek. 37:26; cf. Jer. 31:32), but P employs the same term to indicate that the promises of the oldest covenant in his scheme, the one made with Noah, still hold good (cf. Isa. 54:10).

And what does this covenant promise? (*a*) All flesh will not be cut off again by flood waters, and (*b*) the world itself will never return to chaos (9:11). In this yes to creation, God guarantees the existence of natural and human history. This promise cannot and will not be undone by catastrophes, for example, a worldwide flood or the Exile to Babylon, nor can the mistakes, corruption, or revolt of man annul it.

The specific promises of the everlasting covenant with Abraham will occupy us below. Suffice it to say here that this covenant differs from that with Noah in that its promises relate only to Israel, and in that its sign (circumcision) is not something like the rainbow placed in nature by God, but it is part of the willing assent of Abraham to the covenant (17:10).[10] Although circumcision had been practiced in Israel long before the Exile, P's account of the Abrahamic covenant elevated it to a new height of significance:[11] Circumcision must be practiced forever in Israel, even if such practice evokes the ridicule and disapproval of Israel's Babylonian captors, who did not circumcise their sons, or of the peoples surrounding Palestine, who gave up the practice at about this time. Circumcision, like Sabbath keeping, was a mark of Israel's identity—and faithfulness. Note with what alacrity—on the same day! (vv. 23 and 26)—Abraham circumcised himself, Ishmael, the slaves born in his house, those acquired for money, and all the men of his household (v. 23). Exactly eight days after Isaac's birth Abraham circumcised him as well (21:4). Prompt circumcision is part of Abraham's perfect obedience (17:1).

GOD'S REMEMBERING IN THE PRIESTLY WRITER

No matter how sure and universal the covenant with Noah or how independent from any human participation its validity, might not some in exile have thought even so that God had forgotten them (cf. Lam. 5:20; Ps. 74:18, 22; and Isa. 49:14–15) and that all hope was in vain? For such a crisis P pointed to the rainbow as a sign—for God—of the everlasting covenant. It is a mnemonic device to help him remember the covenant.

The term *remember* is something of a favorite of P's. When God *remembered* Noah and all the beasts and the cattle with

---

10. See Michael V. Fox, "The Sign of the Covenant: Circumcision in the Light of the Priestly 'ôt Etiologies," *RB* 81 (1974) : 588.
11. Ezekiel did not yet know the new significance of circumcision. The phrase "uncircumcised in heart and flesh" (44:7–9) comes from a secondary stratum.

him (8:1), the result was the subsiding of the waters and the safe landing of the ark. God also heard the groaning of Israel in Egypt and *remembered* his covenant with Abraham, with Isaac, and with Jacob (Exod. 2:24; cf. 6:5 and Lev. 26:42). As the following chapters in Exodus make clear, God's remembering of his covenant is not an abstract phenomenon. Remembering his covenant means the raising of a Moses, the besting of Pharaoh, and the liberation of Israel from Egypt.

In both Exod. 2:24 and 6:5, P states that God remembered his people when they were in a foreign land. Precisely when he had seemed to be most forgetful, he did remember after all. P would have the exiles understand the rainbow as the "string tied around Yahweh's finger" that would never let him forget the covenant with Noah. Life and the world are therefore sure.

THE COVENANT WITH ABRAHAM IN P

The everlasting covenant with Abraham went well beyond a promise of fertility or a new name that marked the patriarch's new status. God's principal promise in chap. 17 was "to be God to you and to your seed after you" (v. 7). The reference to "seed after you" is P's way of making vivid the ongoing validity of the covenant for his audience, which was of course Abraham's seed, though it lived in Babylonian exile. The sentence "I will be God to you" is called the "covenant formula" by many Old Testament scholars. It appears primarily in late texts and is usually accompanied by a second clause: "You shall be my people."[12] For our purposes, however, it seems more useful to call it the "God promise." One fulfillment of this God promise came in the Exodus from Egypt, when Yahweh demonstrated once and for all what it means for him to be Israel's God (Exod. 6:6–7; cf. Lev. 11:45; 23:33; 26:45; and Num. 15:41). P may have found in this fulfillment of the God promise reason to hope for a similar fulfillment for exilic Israel. In Exōd. 29:43–44, P reports that God would "meet" with Israel at the tent of meeting so that he

---

12. See Rudolf Smend, *Die Bundesformel,* Theologische Studien 68 (Zürich: EVZ Verlag, 1963).

could consecrate the tent, the altar, and Aaron and his sons (that is, the tabernacle, the sacrificial system, and the priesthood). His citation of Yahweh continues in v. 45: "And I will dwell among the people of Israel, and will be their God." Thus in, or via, his dwelling with Israel in the sanctuary Yahweh would also fulfill the promise to be the God for his people.

The third way in which this God promise manifests itself in P appears already in Genesis 17: "I will give to you, and to your descendants after you, the land of your sojournings, all the land of Canaan, for an everlasting possession; and I will be their God" (v. 8).[13] The descendants of Abraham are explicitly identified here as the corecipients of the promise: they will have everlasting possession of the land and thereby Yahweh will be their God.

But the promised land is only the land of Abraham's sojournings. By the term *sojournings* P recognized that the patriarchs never really occupied the land as owners.[14] In fact, the only piece of land owned and occupied by the patriarchs was the burial cave in the field of Machpelah (Genesis 23). Nevertheless, since the *original* recipients of the promise were sojourners, it is clear that such sojourners—or should we say exiles?—can be recipients of the land promise (cf. Gen. 28:1–4).

In P's account of the call of Moses Yahweh announced that the promise of land would be fulfilled for the people of Moses' day (v. 8). But the Exodus generation did not, in fact, get to occupy the land. Despite their repeated resistance (Exod. 6:9; 14:10, 15; 16:2–3), God spared the people until the incident with the spies, but then he decreed, "And of all your number, numbered from twenty years old and upward, who have murmured against me, not one shall come into the land where I swore I would make you dwell" (Num. 14:29–30). Yet the land promise was not annulled. God committed himself to it even in his last command to Moses to go up and see the land which he had given to the

---

13. On the land promise in P see Elliger, "Sinn und Ursprung," 121–43; and R. Kilian, "Die Hoffnung auf Heimkehr in der Priesterschrift," *BibLeb* (1966) : 39–51.
14. For the patriarchs as sojourners see Gen. 17:8; 23:4; 28:4; 36:7; 37:1; 47:9; and Exod. 6:4.

people of Israel (Num. 27:12; cf. 20:12). Moses looked into the land not just with longing but with confidence, since he knew that the promise stood fast. The second generation in the wilderness, that finally did get the land, was one which in distinction to their ancestors trusted in God. Joshua is held up by P as the one who never faltered in his belief that God would give the land (Num. 14:6–7; Deut. 34:9). Exilic Israel is implicitly urged by P to mimic Joshua's faith and that of the second generation in the wilderness, who walked in perfection and the land was theirs (Deut. 34:9). So Yahweh had once fulfilled the God promise; so would he fulfill it again.

THE NEW DEAL BEGINS: THE CALL OF MOSES

How the events of Exodus and Sinai are the fulfillment of the patriarchal covenant becomes clear in a comparison of Genesis 17 and Exodus 6. In the latter passage we read of the covenant Yahweh established with Abraham, Isaac, and Jacob to give them the land (Exod. 6:4). That covenant, says Yahweh, has now been remembered (v. 5), and the oath promising land to the patriarchs will be kept by giving it to the Exodus generation (v. 8). God's whole nature and identity, his name Yahweh (v. 8; cf. Exod. 12:12), are the guarantee that makes the promise sure.

P divided history into periods, each having its distinctive name for God. In the earliest times, when God's activities in creation and flood concerned the whole world and all of humanity, P employed the generic term for the deity, Elohim. When a new stage began with the covenant with Israel's ancestor Abraham, God assumed a new name to mark his new role as the promiser to Israel. He called himself El Shaddai (Gen. 17:1; cf. 28:3; 35:11; 48:3). The call of Moses begins another new period in P's history, a period that witnessed not only the Exodus from Egypt and the march toward the land but also the institution of the tabernacle, the priesthood, and the sacrificial system. The events beginning with the Exodus are the ones which disclose God's final identity, his name. We might paraphrase: "I am Yahweh. My true identity is that of liberator from Egyptian burdens and bondage. Hence you can count on everything I say."[15]

The name Yahweh plays a crucial role in the subsequent recognition formulas ("You shall know that I am Yahweh"), which disclose key emphases in P's theology. When Moses reported his call to th people, for example, his use of the recognition formula made the Exodus the *means* by which Yahweh became known and the *content* of Israel's knowledge of God: "I am Yahweh, and I will bring you out from under the burdens of the Egyptians . . . and you shall know that I am Yahweh your God, who has brought you out from under the burdens of the Egyptians (Exod. 6:6–7; cf. 16:6 and 29:45–46). Further, Yahweh's attack on the Egyptians at the time of the Exodus and his getting glory over Pharaoh, his chariots, and his riders led even the Egyptians to recognize who he was. These and subsequent recognition formulas disclosed that Yahweh is known only via his gracious actions on and for Israel. Yahweh's actions for Israel in providing them with quails and manna, for example, led to a recognition of his identity (Exod. 16:12) as the God who liberates his people (Exod. 16:6). Even keeping the Sabbath (Exod. 31:13) and the festival of booths (Lev. 23:42–43) were to lead people to *recognize* how Yahweh, whose promises are permanently valid, acted concretely for his people in the past.

ARE THE PROMISES STILL VALID?

How could Israel believe that these promises of the everlasting covenants would become realities, that the Exile would, in fact, end? These questions are answered by P in two ways: (*a*) by pointing to previous partial fulfillments of the promises; and (*b*) by describing God's superiority to tyrannical power as it has been manifested in Israel's oppression by Pharaonic Egypt.

15. The call of Moses contains the only passage in which P uses the term *redeem* of God's actions (Exod. 6:6). Redemption is Yahweh's displaying his role as Israel's kinsman in the only way adequate for a people under real bondage: he used significant and sufficient power to set them free.

FULFILLED PROMISES

The partial fulfillments demonstrated the effectiveness of the promise. God remembered Noah even before the covenant with him was established (Gen. 8:1), but the greatest remembrance of all was God's redeeming Israel from Egypt with great acts of war (Exod. 2:24 and 6:5). The command to be fruitful and multiply was fulfilled effectively both in the Toledoth genealogies of Genesis 5 and 10—11, and in the notices that Israel was fruitful and multiplied in Egypt (Gen. 47:27 and Exod. 1:7). This promise of fertility also had a fulfillment within Abraham's lifetime with the birth of Isaac (Gen. 21:1b).

The land promise, too, had had its fulfillment even for the patriarchs, for the land came into their hands at death. So we hear that Abraham buried Sarah in the cave of the field of Machpelah east of Mamre in the land of Canaan. The field and cave were made over to Abraham as a possession for burying by the Hittites (Gen. 23:9 and 19–20). Isaac and Ishmael buried Abraham in the same cave (25:10), and Jacob gave elaborate instructions to his twelve sons that he be buried at Machpelah (49:30). He also recounted how "they" had buried Abraham and Sarah there, as well as Isaac and Rebekah, and how he had buried Leah (49:31). Jacob's wishes were carried out to the letter by his sons, who brought his body from Egypt to the land of Canaan for burial (50:12–13). The promise of land also had a fulfillment for that wilderness generation that finally entered Palestine with Joshua. These fulfillments demonstrated the power inherent in the promise. If the word of promise had been effective for the patriarchs and the wilderness generation, should not one expect it to be effective also in the Exile? Or could the power of the Babylonian gods or the kings of the Neo-Babylonian Empire thwart God's word of promise?

YAHWEH'S SUPERIORITY TO
TYRANNICAL POWER

The Priestly work deals with this last question by spelling out how superior Yahweh was to the most fearsome enemy power:

the Pharaoh of the Exodus. The plagues in P describe a contest between God and Pharaoh to see who has the greatest power or glory.[16] So pervasive is this approach in P that the demand for the release from Egypt is never mentioned in the course of the plagues themselves (but see 6:11 and 7:2). The climax of P's contest account comes in Yahweh's word at the crossing of the Reed Sea: "I will harden Pharaoh's heart, and he will pursue them (= Israel) and I will get glory over Pharaoh and all his host" (14:4; cf. v. 18).[17] In the end, not one Egyptian was left, but the Israelites paraded through the Reed Sea on dry ground (14:28–29). The Exodus battle, then, was a tournament that determined once and for all whose was the glory.

P illustrates Yahweh's superior power in several ways. First, he tends to heighten the miraculous element in the plague accounts and therefore heighten the degree of Yahweh's victory. When Aaron's rod was cast down before Pharaoh, it became a dragon (*tannîn*, Exod. 7:9), whereas earlier tradition had spoken of Moses' rod that became a snake (*naḥaš*, Exod. 4:2–5 and 7:15). According to J, Yahweh had told Moses to take water from the Nile and pour it on the ground so that it would become blood and verify Moses' credentials to his own people (Exod. 4:9). This *sign* becomes the first *plague* in P. Moreover, the plague involved not only the Nile, whose fish had died according to J when Yahweh struck the water, but all the canals, ponds, rivers, and pools of Egypt, and even the sap in the trees and the water in the springs (Exod. 7:19). A heightening of the miraculous may also be seen in P's description of the Reed Sea crossing, with water piled up on both sides like walls.

An even more striking demonstration of Yahweh's superiority is the contest between Pharaoh's magicians and Aaron. The magicians represented on the one hand the bureaucracy of an impos-

16. The hardening of Pharaoh's heart in P gives Yahweh the opportunity to do more miracles (Exod. 11:9). See Brevard S. Childs, *Exodus*, OTL (Philadelphia: Westminster Press, 1974), pp. 170–75.

17. Yahweh also got glory for himself when fire came out and devoured Nadab and Abihu, who offered unholy fire (Lev. 10:2). Thus Yahweh has power over external threats (Pharaoh and the Egyptians) and over internal threats (Nadab and Abihu).

ing world power (cf. Dan. 2:10), but their wisdom and magic were also subtle covers for hostile divine powers (cf. Exod. 12:12). At first they matched the power of Aaron. When Aaron cast down his rod so that it might become a dragon, the magicians too turned their rods into dragons by their secret arts. Aaron's rod then devoured those of the magicians, thus hinting at Yahweh's ultimate victory (Exod. 7:11–12).

In turning water into blood (see above) the magicians matched Aaron a second time by their secret arts, that is by their quasi-divine powers. Though the plague was already nationwide before the magicians tried to match Moses and Aaron (Exod. 7:21b), P seems undisturbed by this logical difficulty. Similarly the magicians could bring up frogs in the next plague, just as Aaron had done, though the frogs were already nationwide (Exod. 8:5–7). The plague of frogs, in any case, marked the apex of the magicians' power. When they tried to bring up gnats in the third plague, they—and so their secret arts and the gods who stood behind them—failed (8:16–19). The magicians confessed, "This is the finger of God."

They faced, however, one final indignity. In the sixth plague Moses threw ashes skyward and they became boils breaking out in sores on man and beast—including the magicians (Exod. 9:11)! So the magicians passed from the scene in disgrace and implicitly conceded the victory to Yahweh. His was the glory![18]

THE NEW LIFE PRESCRIBED: SINAI

Sinai plays a central role in P's history and theology. And yet, how different is P's Sinai from that of the Deuteronomists, for whom Sinai/Horeb was the place where God gave the retributive covenant with its threatening curses (Deut. 29:20; cf. Lev. 26:25).

---

18. P has another context in which he refers to God's glory: episodes from Israel's everday life in the wilderness (Exod. 16:10; Num. 14:10; 16:19; 42; and 20:6) . See Westermann, "Die Herrlichkeit Gottes in der Priesterschrift," *Wort-Gebot-Glaube*, ed. H. J. Stoebe (Zürich: Zwingli Verlag, 1970) , pp. 227–49. These episodes show that it is one and the same God who met Israel on the sacred mountain, in the tabernacle, and in historical events. Like his fellow priest from the Exile, Ezekiel, P proposed that wholeness *in all things* would result from God's glorious presence in the world.

P solved the problem of broken covenant by restricting the term *covenant* to those unilateral promises made to Noah and Abraham and by giving Sinai a different meaning for Israel's faith.[19] At Sinai Yahweh prescribed the ideal cultic community in which he would graciously dwell with his people and in which they would serve him with a proper priesthood and a proper sacrificial system. In such a community the promises inherent in the everlasting covenants would be realized, and the community's institutions would make possible a blessed and an ongoing life.

YAHWEH DWELLS WITH HIS PEOPLE

P begins his ordering of the cult with the tabernacle. When plans for it were to be given, the glory of Yahweh settled on Mount Sinai, and the cloud covered the mountain for six days. On the seventh, climactic day (Exod. 24:16; cf. Gen. 2:2), God called Moses up the mountain (Exod. 24:15b–18) and gave him detailed prescriptions for the construction of the tabernacle and its furnishings (Exod. 25—27, 30) according to a pattern, or *tabnît,* shown Moses by God (Exod. 25:9, 40; cf. 26:30). Because of the prescriptions written in Exodus 25—27, 30, we might say that exilic Israel itself now had possession of the *tabnît,* thus making possible the tabernacle's reerection.

When the tabernacle was completed on New Year's Day (Exod. 40·1 and 17; cf. Gen. 8:13), the cloud and the glory of Yahweh, which had appeared prior to Moses' receiving the instructions to build, covered the tent of meeting and filled the tabernacle. Thus P stressed the importance of the tabernacle by punctuating both the beginning and the end of its construction with an appearance of the glory of Yahweh. The tabernacle (*miškān*) was simply indispensable. It made possible the practice of Israel's cult, but it was also the means by which God's dwelling (*šākan*) among his people took place (Exod. 25:8). This sanctuary is also called the tent of meeting. Whatever the historical roots of this name, for P it designated the place where "I will meet with you,

19. See Walther Zimmerli, "Sinaibund und Abrahambund," *Gottes Offenbarung,* TBü 19 (München: Christian Kaiser, 1963), pp. 205–16.

to speak there to you" (Exod. 29:42). The community that gath-
ers around the tent of meeting (*'ōhel mō'ēd*), where God meets
with his people (*y'd*, Niphal), is called the congregation (*'ēdâ*).
P employed the archaic term *škn* to indicate that God's presence
with his people is not to be taken for granted or understood as
the concrete abiding of Yahweh in his shrine.[20] God's freedom
and transcendence are carefully maintained. P makes very clear
that God's dwelling with his people is. the fulfillment of the
promise to be their God (Exod. 29:45) and that it is the goal
behind the Exodus itself.

The sanctuary was the place from which God directed his
people from time to time already in the wilderness (cf. Num.
10:1–13). That this direction was not limited to the period of the
wilderness leaders, Moses and Aaron, is demonstrated by the
accounts of their deaths and the orderly transition of leadership
from Aaron to Eleazar (Num. 20:22–29) and from Moses to
Joshua (Num. 27:12–23; Deut. 34:1–7, 9). Israel's life goes forward after these events the same as before, except now Moses'
successor Joshua is subject to Eleazar the priest, the leader of
P's cultic community (Num. 27:20–21; per contra Exod. 7:1).
Here we see adumbrated the great power of the priesthood, that
became nearly absolute in postexilic times.

God's dwelling with Israel in the cloud is such an awesome
thing that it prevents even Moses from entering the tent of meeting (Exod. 40:35). The picture of the camp in P illustrates this
sense of holiness or awe by putting the tabernacle in the center
of two concentric rings. In the innermost ring, closest to the
tabernacle, are the Levites to protect and transport the sacred
shrine (Num. 1:47–54). Moses, Aaron, and his sons (Num. 3:38)
occupy the favored eastern position while the other Levitic
groups (Kohathites, Gershonites, and Merarites) occupy the
southern, western, and northern positions respectively (Num.
3:23, 29, 35). The secular tribes are relegated to the second
ring (Num. 2:3–31).

God's dwelling in the midst of the holy camp was not to be
defiled by the presence of lepers (Lev. 13:46), people with a dis-

20. See Cross, "The Tabernacle," *BA* 10 (1947) : 65–68.

charge (Lev. 15), or people who had contact with the dead (Lev. 21:1–12; cf. Num. 5:2–3).[21] Such unclean people cannot coexist with Yahweh in the camp. Israel of wilderness days set an example by driving them out of the camp in obedience to Yahweh's command (Num. 5:4).

In addition to facilitating the meeting between Yahweh and his people, the tabernacle also provided housing for the "testimony" (*'ēdût*), which was contained in the ark (e.g. Exod. 25:16, 21). It seems clear that *'ēdût* refers to the law tablets or Decalogue of the old Sinai covenant (see especially Exod. 31:18 and 34:29).[22] How could there be a Sinai without some kind of document corresponding to the Ten Commandments? But P does not discuss the contents of the *'ēdût* and, significantly, it is not called *běrît*.[23]

In any case, P's ideal for the future worship of Israel involved a return to the cult initiated at Sinai. Back then God met his people in his tabernacle dwelling. That tabernacle housed the law tablets, and in its precincts the sacrifices were carried out by a priesthood legitimated at Sinai. So it once was; so it should be again.

PRIESTS OF THE PAST AND FUTURE

This is not the place to spell out all of P's views on the priesthood and the sacrificial system.[24] According to P the only legitimate priests were Aaron and his sons who had been invested by Moses himself. Far inferior to the priests were the Levites, who were assigned menial tasks (Num. 3—4; 8; 18:2–7). P's account

---

21. These rules may well be late (largely P*), but there is no reason to doubt that they are legitimate inferences drawn from the theology of P*. Cf. also Num. 35:34.

22. Cf. B. Volkwein, "Massoretisches *'ēdût, 'ēdwōt, 'ēdōt*—'Zeugnis' oder 'Bundesbestimmungen,'" *BZ* 13 (1969) : 18–40.

23. The possible bridges between P's cultic emphases at Sinai and the old covenantal traditions have been discussed by Delbert Hillers, *Covenant: The History of a Biblical Idea* (Baltimore: Johns Hopkins Press, 1969), pp. 162–66.

24. See the excellent short discussions and bibliographies in *IDBSup*: B. A. Levine, "Priests," pp. 687–90; J. Milgrom, "Atonement, Day of," 82–83; and idem, "Sacrifices and Offerings, OT," pp. 763–71.

of the rebellion of Korah demonstrates the fatal consequences of any attempt to encroach upon the privileges of the sons of Aaron (Num. 16; cf. 18:7).

The service for the ordination of the priests was prescribed at Sinai (Exod. 29:1–37), and it was first carried out, also at Sinai, in obedient response to God's command (Lev. 8—9). So important were the questions of legitimate priesthood and proper sacrifice that P reports remarkable phenomena that accompanied the ordination of the first priests and the carrying out of the initial sacrifices: the appearance of the glory of Yahweh and the kindling of the sacrificial fire by no one less than Yahweh himself (Lev. 9:23–24).

SACRIFICES PAST AND FUTURE[25]

Israel according to P was a sinful people (cf. our discussion of the sins of the people and their leaders), and P was aware that the people would constantly come into contact with the unclean world in daily life. It should come as no surprise, therefore, that expiation and purification receive major emphasis in the sacrificial system. Much of the Holiness Code (Lev. 17—26), which was eventually incorporated into P, is concerned with the cultic and ethical holiness of the people before God.

The purpose of the blood in the frequent sin offerings (*ḥaṭṭā't*) was to purge the sanctuary and its holy furnishings. By such offerings the priests cleansed the sacred areas that had been polluted by physical impurity (Lev. 12—15) or by inadvertent offense to God (Lev. 4). Presumptuous, high-handed sins, on the other hand, could only be purged, at least in the final form of P, by the annual rite of purgation for the sanctuary and the nation, that is, the Day of Atonement (Lev. 16). The slain bull and goat on this day were to purge the shrine of the physical *pollution* effected by Israel's brazen sins (Lev. 16:16, 19). Without such

---

25. The question of which parts of the sacrificial regulations belong to P^g and which to P^s remains, now as before, highly disputed. We believe that what is said below about the sacrificial system and its purposes would have made sense to the priestly tradents already in the Exile, regardless of when the specific texts went through their final editing.

purgations the pollution would adhere to the sanctuary and amass until God could not longer abide there. By driving away the "scapegoat" on the Day of Atonement, the *guilt* for the people's iniquities, which had been transferred to the goat (Lev. 16:22), was also carried off. Thus the slain *ḥaṭṭā't* purged the sanctuary from pollution while the living *ḥaṭṭā't* carried off the people's sins.

Purgation and forgiveness[26] are not prerequisites to God's renewed dwelling in the tabernacle and land; they are, rather, necessary requirements that must be carried through if that dwelling is to have an abiding future. The sins of individuals threaten the community as a whole since the pollution of individual sins left unpurged leads finally to the destruction of the community itself. The following exhortations in the Holiness Code presumably express common priestly understanding of the consequences of sin's pollution: "You shall keep my statutes and my ordinances and do none of these abominations . . . lest the land vomit you out, when you defile it, as it vomited out the nation that was before you" (Lev. 18:26 and 28).

CONCLUSION

P's new community is to be shaped after that one formed at Sinai, whose chief characteristics were a tabernacle in which Yahweh dwelled, a proper priesthood, and a proper sacrificial system. This new community is to be brought about only by the force inherent in promises from the past, the covenants with Noah and Abraham. P showed in numerous ways how the promises of these covenants had been effective in the past and why they could be trusted in exile. He urged the exiles to maintain their identity by keeping the Sabbath and practicing circumcision.

Each year Israel remembered at the Passover what Yahweh had done in Egypt (Exod. 12:14; 13:9), but they would also be led by the message of P to expect Yahweh to repeat his saving actions, so that both Israel and the nations among whom they lived would

26. On forgiveness see J. J. Stamm's discussion of *slḥ* in *Theologisches Handwörterbuch zum Alten Testament,* ed. E. Jenni and C. Westermann (Munich: C. Kaiser, 1966), vol. 2, col. 150–60.

recognize Yahweh as the mighty God, who gets glory for himself in his historical deeds. A reader of P would know what good things happen to Israel and what bad things to their oppressors when God remembers his covenant. And God could not forget his covenant with Noah and Abraham despite his apparent forgetfulness in P's day. The rainbow, Yahweh's gracious addition to the created order, would inevitably bring his memory of the covenant to life. P ends his narrative with old Israel on the verge of the land and full of hope, and that is *where* and *how* he wanted his audience to understand themselves as well.

Conclusion—

Light for *Our* Exile[1]

Israel's experience of and reaction to exile greatly illuminate our own situation in faith and culture. For us too the old answers no longer hold; our optimistic expectations are contradicted by our increasingly depressing experiences. One can be in exile without ever leaving the land.

Many of the apparent bases for faith have slipped away in our day. Secularism rules not only as a result of post-Enlightenment philosophy but also because of our preoccupation with things and the dominant technological thinking. The advice to Job, "Curse God and die," seems quaint; we are more inclined to think clearly and have no hope (Camus). Frantic attempts to prove God's existence through miracles or to ground faith in a precritical view of Scripture indicate just how pervasive the silence of God has become. No one escapes this exile.

The institutions of Western life have also failed miserably. Science and technology have not made the world more peaceful, nor have "the best and the brightest" been able to recreate our cities, devise workable social programs, or even manage themselves. The institutional church shares in this failure. Long gone are the days when it was part of the growth society. When we sing, "Like a mighty army moves the church of God," our contemporaries reply, "You've got to be kidding." It's not that the church doesn't have its share of good and dedicated people, but

---

1. I am indebted to Douglas John Hall, "Towards an Indigenous Theology of the Cross," *Int* 30 (1976): 153–68, for stimulating many insights into the diagnosis of our exile.

as an institution it often seems excessively obsessed with survival, hell-bent on compromise, or just trivial. As sociologist Thomas Luckmann observes, "The decrease in traditional church religion may be seen as a consequence of the shrinking relevance of the values institutionalized in church religion for the integration and legitimation of everyday life in modern society."[2]

Life itself is threatened in this exile, not least by the ongoing arms race. We have reached the limits of growth and the end of cheap energy. We suffer from the depletion of all natural resources. Inflation robs people on fixed or moderate income of a chance for a decent and comfortable life.

Our exile is God's judgment. Israel had to learn that 587 could not be averted by military alliances or fighting to the last man. DtrH made clear that Israel's fall was the inevitable and justified result of a centuries-long pursuit of "other gods." We may have difficulty imagining ourselves bowing down to a statue of wood or stone, but we surely know *that* idolatry which fears, loves, and trusts in something or someone other than God. Such "other gods" we know well; their name is legion.

The criticisms cited in the above paragraphs could be debated, I suppose. My hope in citing them was to use them primarily as symptoms of our idolatry (fill in your own symptoms if you will). If we see our problems in deep enough dimensions, we will recognize that they can't be solved by a little tinkering with the dials, a few new programs, a couple new faces, a remodeled liturgy, or by submerging ourselves in activism and programs. Jeremiah's temple address warned against those who committed flagrant sins and then ran to Yahweh's house with the cry "We are delivered." Cures don't come easily or cheaply.

This exile is home for the time being. The problems we face now will not go away easily; they might not go away at all. The struggle to find an authoritative basis for the faith promises to be with us for the duration. The energy crisis will not disappear with the discovery of a few new oil fields, probably not even with a new kind of energy. The power brokers in the world will not be able to ignore the legitimate demands of the Third World.

2. Thomas Luckmann, *The Invisible Religion* (New York: Macmillan Co., 1967), p. 39.

And those demands can only be fulfilled if the power and wealth in fact change hands. Surely such exilic problems will last for at least seventy years!

We need to follow Jeremiah's advice and make ourselves at home in this exile. It won't do for us to deny the challenges to faith in the modern world or to hope for a day with easier social-political questions. They can only get worse. We need to seek the peace of this city, to pray for our own enemy's prosperity, to know that here and now is the arena of our vocation.

The truth of the sketches of the new day in Ezekiel or in Second Isaiah does not depend on whether or not streams ever gurgled out of a newly constructed temple or whether the Israelites marched home on a superhighway with Yahweh coming along both fore and aft. The power of these writings was first of all that they helped Israel to maintain the faith during the Exile, to trust Yahweh's promise, and to maintain the community when everything seemed lost. This was a theology which affirmed the victory even when empirical death and sin continued. When God seemed most hidden—there, in exile—they spoke of his revelation.

Exile is a time for maintaining identity. In the sixth century B.C. practicing circumcision and keeping the Sabbath apparently made a lot of waves; such observance was also the *articulus stantis et cadentis ecclesiae*—the issue that would decide whether the community would stand or fall. This chapter is a call not to curse the darkness but to be a light in its midst. No call to abandon the church, but to confess as church our sinfulness and to cling ever more obediently to the word of forgiveness. No call away from the struggle for social justice and world peace, but a call to greater efforts, for more daring programs, for living "as if" the world's social and political evils can be conquered—even if they can't.

Exile is a time for hope, not triumphalism. The book of Jeremiah knew the difference between these two terms. To say only no to exile is triumphalism; to say only yes is hopelessness. To say yes and no is to affirm the judgment, to recognize this exilic existence as our real vocation, and yet to confess and actualize the transforming power of the Promiser.

What hope? For Second Isaiah creation was not just a thing of the past; it was a guarantee of Yahweh's present power and a blueprint for what he would do with barren deserts and physically disabled people in a new era. God's presence with his people, according to Ezekiel 47, would bring fertility to the Judean desert and life to the Dead Sea. You have to visit these sites to understand the radicality of Ezekiel's promise! Must not we Christians proclaim such hope in our exile? John's gospel tells us that rivers of living water flow from the heart of Jesus. His body is now the temple of God in which God chooses to dwell. From the pierced side of this crucified one flow rivers of blood and water. What kinds of renewal do we expect in the church, in society, and in the world from this presence?

Exile is a time for new obedience. The more exuberant the exilic gospel described in this book—of a new covenant in Jeremiah, of God's all-transforming presence in Ezekiel, of a new exodus and procession to Zion in Second Isaiah—the more we saw also the call to a new life of obedience. That new life too is God's gift, made possible by that acquitting and forgiving word of God which brought his debilitating and demoralizing accusation against Israel to an end.

And don't be surprised if the shape of that obedience is suffering. As we disentangle the faith from the triumphalism of our culture, we will be called again to be the servant of Yahweh. Only in such a role—as those who suffer *with* others in exile and even *for* them—will we be God's witness, his light to the nations. Our suffering may come as we take cognizance of our "limits," as we dismantle our political and economic hegemony, as we identify with the poverty and pain of many a modern Lazarus and recognize that we share with them a common lot: we too are beggars. Through our repentant servant shape others can perhaps learn what God is up to in the world. As P insisted, Yahweh's name is revealed in and via his liberation of servants; in Second Isaiah's view, Yahweh is the one who vindicates suffering slaves.

In the introduction we spoke of Israel turning its problems into theological opportunities. Jeremiah bought land just when the whole country was changing hands, confident that someday again the promise of land would have its fruition. The poet in

Lamentations saw Jerusalem at a nadir, with foxes prowling as curses on Zion's height, and precisely then he dared to say, "Yet, Yahweh is my king . . ." Our exile too can be the opportune time for bold assertions of faith.

We need variety in the faith too. Second Isaiah and P both hoped for the future, but their differences could hardly have been more pronounced. P banked on the old promises; Second Isaiah proclaimed God's new thing. The variety in their message means that different messages are needed by different people. Spiritual hunger must be relieved by the appropriate food. But the other side of variety is complementarity. Divergent responses to exile can together form a greater testimony to God than any one of these responses by itself. This is one of the great contributions of the renewed stress on canon today, and it is a great prod to ecumenical dialogue and cooperation.

Exile was and is a catalyst for translating the faith. A Second Isaiah could take the traditions of the old exodus and the old Zion processions and say that God's word guaranteed a new exodus and a new trip to Zion. God's presence had always been affirmed in Israel, but in the hands of an Ezekiel it became really good news for folks in exile. Biblical theology has been defined as describing what the Bible meant and what it might mean today. To proclaim the faith of the fathers in the language of the children cannot be done in only a few lines, and especially not alone. But it can and must be done.

Exile for Christians is a time for viewing the world through the eyes of the cross. Such a view bears witness to the continuity between Old Testament and New, between promise and fulfillment. But it also helps us to appropriate the old exilic solution for our time. Do not our hearts burn within us when we read Second Isaiah's oracles of salvation? "Fear not, I have redeemed you, I have called you by name, you are mine." Do not they burn because we hear the same word from the cross and from the empty tomb?

But exile is also temptation. There is the temptation to say yes to all religious answers without discrimination, to offer no judgment in exile or announce easy deliverance from it, to curse the darkness or ignore it. There is the temptation to simplify theology and its problems, to speak lies on God's behalf (Job 13:7–8), to think we have to defend him by overlooking theology's blind corners or unresolved tensions. There is also the temptation to react to our fractured community by an inward trip to isolated individualism.

Exile is a time for praying to Yahweh who is both king and enemy at the same time (Lamentations). Exile is a time for examination of ourselves, our community, our country, and our church, for seeing their present state as judgment, and for turning to God with heart, soul, and mind (the Deuteronomistic History). Exile is a time for affirming our exile, yet refusing to be overcome by it (Jeremiah). Exile is a time for preserving the old promises *and* for translating them into a meaningful message for today (Ezekiel). Exile is a time for celebrating and proclaiming God's power to save (Second Isaiah). Exile is a time for returning to the old promises and for restoring, if need be, the old institutions, so that we can move into the future, knowing full well that God's memory of his promises is our only hope (P).

Exile is a time for . . . But these paragraphs must only be a down payment on the hermeneutical task. The full harvest must come from the many voices who speak for God. He, now as before, is the center of life in exile and in the land—and beyond.

Scripture Index

155